Smile Inside

Experiential Activities
for Self-Awareness
Ages 14-15

Vanessa Lee

Smile Inside
Experiential Activities for Self-Awareness Ages 14-15
© 2013 Vanessa Lee
All rights reserved.

Published simultaneously in the United States and Australia.

Cover and book design by Alfred Abraham
Graphic illustrations by Laura Sullivan

Library of Congress Control Number: 2011901857
ISBN: 978-0-9895111-4-8
First edition
10 9 8 7 6 5 4 3 2

Prevention
Publications
www.preventionpublications.com

*In memory of Mr. Haas, an unforgettable teacher
who inspired me to write this book.*

Contents

smile inside

smile inside

smile inside

Preface

As a professional who works in the fields of education and welfare, I have observed a critical need for young people to develop the necessary awareness to understand themselves and to cope with life's challenges. Disrespectful behavior toward others is frequently an indication of frustrations and an inability to cope with emotions or address issues occurring in their lives. For a maladjusted individual, good behavior and respect for all is often merely a result of the control authority can force upon him or her for limited periods of time. Good behavior needs to be genuine and a reflection of what's occurring inside.

The *Smile Inside* philosophy is based on a very simple concept: people thrive when they're emotionally balanced, self-aware, and authentic with themselves and others. Having a healthy sense of self-worth and the tools necessary to manage themselves will also help young people find happiness and success in their personal lives.

In order for young people to achieve this, they must be given the opportunity to gain insight about themselves: their behaviors, their feelings, their minds, and their motivations. It is imperative to help youth acquire healthy senses of self and cater to their social and emotional needs. When we support them in developing the skills and awareness needed to overcome setbacks, we help prevent problems like suicide, depression, anxiety, eating disorders, addiction, and abuse, which are all prevalent today.

If young people can strengthen their convictions to remain authentic and stay true to themselves throughout life, they are less likely to be affected by unhealthy influences and less tempted to make wrong turns on their journeys. Coming to a deeper understanding of self and one's relationship with the world is essential in order to maintain sound emotional and mental health and live responsibly. My wish is that the well-being of youth becomes a priority in every community and country across the world.

"We must be the change we wish to see in the world."

——Mahatma Gandhi

Acknowledgments

When I was a teenager, I was lucky enough to be selected to attend a number of camps that profoundly influenced me. I also took a few elective courses in high school that focused on personal development. These experiences helped me gain self-awareness, self-respect, confidence, and some understanding of how I fit into and could relate to the world. Being a teenager wasn't easy and I swore I would never forget how challenging it could be or the experiences that truly made a difference in my life. At fourteen, I started to record all my favorites, vowing someday, in some way, I would see to it that as many teens as possible would have access to the same life-changing experiences.

I am very grateful to the individuals and organizations who saw the importance of developing the whole person and inspired me to do the work I do today:

- Mr. P. Haas, who introduced me to myself during Humanities, an amazing elective I took in high school that focused on personal development.
- Ms. L. Smith, a teacher who reached so many teens while running programs like Youth to Youth and one of my favorites, Quest.
- Mr. G. Roth, my student council advisor who gave a friend and me free rein to coordinate a weekend leadership retreat and other programs for our peers. What amazing opportunities for a teenager!
- Project P.A.N.D.A. (Prevent and Neutralize Drug and Alcohol Abuse, www.projectpanda.com)
  - Project P.A.N.D.A is a prevention, education, and outreach program under the umbrella of the Community Health Center in Akron, Ohio. I first went on one of their weekend retreats when I was in middle school; it was a fantastic experience.
- OASC (Ohio Association of Student Councils, www.oasc-oh.org)
  - OASC's goals include promoting student council programs and providing education through conferences and camps. Their participants gain valuable leadership skills and insight into what it means to be active citizens in their communities.
- OTI (Ohio Teen Institute, www.ohioti.com)
  - OTI's main mission is to empower young people to become resilient, responsible leaders who make a positive impact on the world. I adored being part of their motivational camps and introducing them to others.
- Support Inc. (Teleteen, Akron, Ohio)
  - Teleteen was a suicide crisis line specifically for teenagers. I valued the training and experience.
- CARE (Creating Active and Reflective Educators)
  - At Ohio University, I participated in a program that gave an alternative route to teaching certification. It examined effective, unorthodox methods of teaching and gave students access to extensive field experience. Thank you to all the professors in the College of Education and Human Services who created the program and have kept it going. I'm also grateful to the creative teachers who open their classroom doors to CARE students year after year.

Since graduating from college, I have developed a passion for engaging young people in personal development experiences. I have continued to collect, test, revise, and create activities that meet the needs of today's youth. Countless people have assisted me along the way. I wish I could mention every one of them. In addition, I wrote a number of these activities from memory many years after I experienced them. I am grateful to those individuals who have unknowingly contributed to this resource with their creative ideas and words of wisdom.

Heartfelt thanks to:

- Vivekananda Yoga School (S-VYASA), for teaching me about "monkey mind" and self-discipline.
- The students and staff of Daylesford Secondary College from 2003-2006, for being cooperative and helpful in my pursuits of conducting trials, revising, and retesting programs.
- Karla and Lou, for your encouragement.
- Chelsea, for being the ultimate intern.
- My favorite sister, Sam, for testing activities and giving me valuable advice throughout the process.
- Shyam, for your support.
- Above all, God, for everything.

Vanessa Lee 2013

smile inside

Introduction

Smile Inside encourages participants to become masters of their own minds and behaviors—skills that are necessary for a smooth transition into adulthood. This resource gives young people access to self-improvement opportunities packaged in various ways to help them become self-aware and grow into the best people they choose to be.

The methodology used for this resource in its entirety is based on an experiential learning cycle model originally proposed by David A. Kolb in 1975 with Ralph Fry and expanded upon in Kolb's 1984 book *Experiential Learning: Experience as the Source of Learning and Development*. Kolb based his work on the philosophy of John Dewey, a leading pioneer in progressive education. Within the experiential learning cycle, individuals participate in activities after which they're encouraged to reflect on and communicate their realizations. After making conclusions, participants are given more opportunities to test their newly formed principles through further structured experiences. In essence, this teaching method causes participants to revise their prior understandings as they encounter new information in order to deepen their comprehension of themselves, others, and the world. They improve their abilities to reflect and evolve, which are essential in the process of personal growth. In addition, many of the activities utilize active learning, cooperative learning, and inquiry-based learning—all student-centered approaches in education.

Smile Inside activities challenge individuals to have integrity when dealing with their feelings and minds and advocate empathy, tolerance, and looking past facades when encountering other people. Experiences like these have profound effects on everyone, but in particular, they strengthen support networks for otherwise socially isolated young people. Furthermore, some of the activities help uncover serious problems when participants are given opportunities to disclose personal anxieties. Minor or major issues may be revealed, and these moments allow the facilitators to identify where support or intervention may be needed.

The journey varies for every participant, but all outcomes are significant because the process allows individuals to come to realizations about themselves and others that may not necessarily occur without the experiences the activities provide. The Esprit de Corps through Service Learning module (p. 135) gives participants the opportunity to explore a social issue that is meaningful to them and to make a positive difference in this area. The *Make a Change Challenge* (p. 150) engages participants in the greater community and instills self-respect. They're given the chance to build productive relationships with others who share their passions and visions. Their achievements lead to renewed faith in their abilities to cope successfully with challenges that come their way.

Using This Handbook

Smile Inside activities can be used to supplement a well-being program or in its entirety as a personal development course. It can also be used to address presenting issues by running a one-day workshop, facilitating a weekend retreat, or choosing relevant activities to meet the needs of your group. The sessions can be conducted by teachers, youth workers, youth group leaders, youth leaders, camp counselors, or anyone who works with young people.

Working through the modules in sequential order is recommended so participants can sharpen the prerequisites needed to enhance their experiences in later modules. The exception to this is *Right Your Rules* (p. 26), which can be conducted in the first or second session after the group has warmed up with a few icebreakers. This activity helps lay the foundation for an emotionally safe environment.

Keep moving forward as long as the participants are proceeding with a firm grasp of the module concepts and putting their refined skills and understandings into practice. You will know your participants best.

Participants

It's best to limit your group to no more than sixteen participants in order to establish a relatively intimate atmosphere. In larger groups young people tend to stay more reserved or use humor or other methods to mask their true feelings or opinions.

Most of the activities can be modified to be developmentally appropriate for participants as young as twelve and can be used with youth up to the age of eighteen under the right conditions. Some even work great with adults! This handbook just recommends activities that have worked well with ages fourteen and fifteen, although maturity levels do fluctuate depending on a number of factors. In ninth grade individuals are forming their self-identities and will positively develop their values, morals, and personal codes of conduct if given the time and guidance to do so properly. This handbook gives more mature participants opportunities for self-analysis and personal improvement. While both *Smile Inside* handbooks explore the same topics, *Smile Inside: Experiential Activities for Self-Awareness Ages 12-14* focuses a little bit more on empathy, optimism, and working well with others.

To maximize the program's impact on the participants' personal growth, revisit the module topics over a two-to three-year period with the same group, if possible.

Materials

Space

The group sessions should take place in a quiet, private room if possible. Conducting activities in a circle promotes attentive listening and cohesiveness but can make some feel vulnerable. If you encounter this, use a circle of tables and chairs or desks; otherwise use chairs alone or cushions on the floor. A few activities require a large, open space that can easily be achieved by pushing everything up against the walls.

smile inside

Visual Aids

Whatever setting you find yourself in, you should have access to a whiteboard, a chalkboard, a writing easel, paper from a roll taped to a wall, or an audiovisual projector using PowerPoint. Some activities require photocopying.

Time

Each activity's estimated duration is based on a group of sixteen participants but it will depend on the depth of conversation. Some will run short, so always have your next activity or a few riddles on hand—look for them in the Problem Solving and Decision Making module (p. 91). The freedom to extend a session at will is always a good thing if the topic is intense or the participants are fully engaged.

Journals

Interactive Journal (p. 9) is an integral part of the facilitator-youth relationship but can only be properly used in a program that goes well beyond just one interaction or a one-day group experience. It will require time and commitment on the facilitator's part, but it is well worth it. This ongoing, written dialogue provides a platform for honest sharing and plays a vital role in helping participants process their feelings and experiences, which, in turn, helps them increase their emotional intelligence.

Choose questions relevant to the topic that the participants can answer in their journals. Encourage them to write their thoughts, feelings, or anything else they would like to share with you, including drawings and poetry. Within each module in this handbook there are relevant quotes that some participants may want to copy into their journals. The journal can also easily be used for taking notes throughout your time together.

Collect the journals at the end of every session if you have concerns about the participants remembering to bring them each time you meet. Otherwise periodically take them home to respond to their entries. Ask questions that challenge each individual to reflect even more deeply, and look for opportunities to provide positive feedback.

One of the benefits of the journal dialogue is that it can uncover serious issues and get help for those who really need support. If you let participants know right away that you'll "keep it confidential unless you reveal that you or someone else is in danger," it may discourage them from totally opening up to you and may even shut them down from the start. If participants ask or do disclose troubling information, explain that you're required by law to report when anyone is in harm's way.

The journals can simply be notebooks with pockets for the handouts or you may want to tailor one to suit your group. Create a customized journal by compiling the handouts you plan to use along with extra pages specifically for journal entries. For your convenience, full-color versions of all the handouts are available for download at www.smileinside.com.au. Alternatively, the participants could build a journal as they go using a binder with plastic pockets.

Being a Facilitator

Ideally, having two facilitators will give the participants the benefit of two minds and more attention, but one can still effectively lead the activities. You can always recruit local university students looking for field experience or youth workers from a local agency who may add value, but ensure they will be present for the duration of the program.

One of the most important responsibilities of a facilitator is to create and maintain a safe and supportive atmosphere. The participants will be more willing to take emotional risks and engage in deep and meaningful conversations and reflections when they feel secure and valued. This foundation must be laid during the first few sessions through extensive icebreakers, activities such as *Right your Rules* (p. 26) or *The Problem with Villains* (p. 30), and inquisitive but private confrontations of any put-downs. If participants are continually rude or defiant, take the time to find out what's really going on with them and help them realize why they're acting that way. Keep in mind that some activities in this handbook give young people the opportunity to disclose personal information that may require intervention. Be sensitive with these participants and immediately help find the support they need by contacting a parent or guardian, or refer them through the appropriate channels to receive assistance from professionals.

Leading these activities is not so much about teaching personal development; it's more about facilitating experiences while assisting the participants to reflect upon their feelings and realizations. The quality of each young person's participation during the activities will influence the depth of his or her realizations, but the facilitator can further enhance the benefits through the processing phase at the end of each activity.

Remind participants of the module topics before or at the conclusion of activities. Be transparent about the fact that every activity is meant to relay a lesson and the more they put into it, the more they will get out of it. Participants can draw many pearls of wisdom from each experience and it's likely they'll come up with some abstract lessons that haven't even crossed your mind. A good way to start any processing session is to ask, "What did this activity teach us?" Then choose some of the suggested questions as a guide. Drawing realizations from the participants will aid in their retention of the concepts being presented.

Ultimately, you want your group to experience the personal rewards that come from achieving *esprit de corps* with others. Esprit de corps is about working in harmony as a group that displays loyalty, enthusiasm, pride, and devotion to its goal. Always stay alert for opportunities that will help the group evolve or help an individual move forward in his or her growth. Point out when the group has stepped up and praise them when they function as a unit.

"Give a man a fish and you feed him for a day.
Teach him how to fish and you feed him for a lifetime."

—Lao Tzu

smile inside

"Give a child a thought; you prepare him for the day.
Teach a child how to think, you prepare him for a lifetime."

—Author Unknown

ICEBREAKERS

In any new group, individuals tend to construct protective shields around themselves. These shields create an ice-like barrier. Icebreakers help to melt participants' fears, making it much easier for them to get to know each other authentically.

Extensive icebreakers give the group time to bond before getting into the more introspective and emotionally challenging activities in later sessions. Fun and laughter are powerful allies in group situations and encourage individuals to reveal their true selves. Participants will share positive experiences from the start of their time together and have a chance to get to know each other better.

The Name Game

Participants will share descriptive characteristics and remember the characteristics and names of peers.

1. Begin by sitting in a circle so the participants can see each other clearly.

2. Explain that everyone needs to come up with an adjective beginning with the first letter of their first name that exemplifies their personality in a positive way. Encourage everyone to help those who are unable to think of one.

3. The following are examples:

   - Active Antonio
   - Brilliant Bobby
   - Confident Chris
   - Delightful Danny
   - Excellent Elizabeth
   - Friendly Fred
   - Grateful Gavin
   - Helpful Hanna
   - Interesting Ian
   - Joyful Justine
   - Kinetic Katie
   - Laughing Liz
   - Magnificent Mark
   - Natural Nancy
   - Optimistic Oliver
   - Pleasant Polly
   - Quirky Quinn
   - Rockin' Rose
   - Sporty Sam
   - Ticklish Teresa
   - Understanding Uma
   - Vivacious Vicki
   - Wonderful William
   - X-citing Xavier
   - Youthful Yasmin
   - Zany Zita

4. The dialogue will make its way around the circle as follows:

   Facilitator: I'm Chilled Chelsea.
   Person 1: This is Chilled Chelsea and I am Jubilant Jessica.
   Person 2: This is Chilled Chelsea, this is Jubilant Jessica, and I am Bright Brian.
   Person 3: This is Chilled Chelsea, she is Jubilant Jessica, he's Bright Brian, and I'm Amazing Alex.

5. The process continues until it's the facilitator's turn once again.

smile inside

The M&M Game

Participants will share personal information with their peers.

materials   one large bag of M&Ms, a visual aid

1. Pass around the bag of M&Ms and have everyone take a handful. Give everyone permission to eat the light-brown and dark-brown ones.

2. Write on the visual aid what the remaining colors mean:

   • Red—Family
   • Yellow—Talents
   • Green—School
   • Blue—Favorites
   • Orange—Interests

3. Have each participant share something about the topic with the group according to the number and color of M&Ms they hold in their hand.

smile inside

Clump

Participants will discover with whom they share common traits and interests.

1. Conduct this activity in a space where participants have plenty of room to move about. Explain the following rules:

   - Categories will be named one at a time (e.g., what they had for breakfast).
   - Everyone needs to form groups with those who have the same response (granola bar, cereal, pancakes, fruit, toast, etc.).
   - Walk and talk in order to form "clumps".
   - Each group will share their common bond with the other groups by announcing it when signaled.

2. Name a category:

   - Favorite food
   - Favorite color
   - Birthday month
   - Sign of the zodiac
   - Eye color
   - Favorite sport to play
   - Favorite sport to watch
   - Toothpaste used

   - Favorite actor
   - Favorite subject in school
   - Favorite fast food
   - Favorite TV show
   - Favorite movie
   - Favorite kind of music
   - Favorite fruit
   - Transportation to school

3. Assist in the formation of groups by helping stragglers find groups and supporting individuals in groups of one.

4. Once everyone has found a clump, signal each group to share aloud in turn.

smile inside

Honey, If You Love Me...

Participants will share descriptive characteristics and remember the characteristics and names of peers.

1. Participants may sit for this activity although it works best when they're standing in a circle. The participants will feel more exposed and vulnerable, making self-control more difficult. Ask a volunteer to stand in the center.

2. Mention that this activity is about practicing restraint and explain the following rules to everyone but direct them at the person in the middle of the circle:

   - You have one chance to make another person smile without touching him or her.
   - The only words you may use are "honey, if you love me, you'd smile!"
   - You may be as comedic in voice inflections and body movements as you wish.
   - Your victim must respond, "Honey, I love you, but I just can't smile" with a straight face. If your victim smiles before, during, or immediately after saying the line, they take your place. If not, you must continue creatively until you get someone to smile.

3. Continue until every participant has had the chance to practice restraint. Congratulate those who were able to maintain self-control under those circumstances.

4. Ask the participants to give examples of, other than holding back laughter, when the skill of restraint might benefit them (when it's important to be polite, when learning in the classroom, when feeling angry, when listening to someone share something important to them, etc.).

smile inside

Personal Shields

Participants will design artistic portrayals of their interests, thoughts, and feelings. They will recognize how and why they may be protective of their personal information.

materials   image of a coat of arms, *Shield* handouts or journals, markers/art supplies, a visual aid

1. Ask the group:

   - What's the first thing that comes to mind when you think of a shield? (E.g., protection, a coat of arms.)
   - What do you know about the decoration of shields in history? (The coat of arms represents a country, university, or family—their emblems, crests, or symbols adorn the fronts of shields.)

2. Show an example of a coat of arms to the group. Explain that traditionally a shield would promote information to others.

3. Their task is to create personalized shields that will help others get to know them better. The shields will also help them discover how they protect themselves.

4. Write these prompts on the visual aid:

   - This is what's special to me...
   - This is what frightens me...
   - I'm looking forward to...
   - I'm loved because...
   - This is negative in my life...
   - This is positive in my life...
   - A special family event is...
   - I was worried when...
   - Here are my favorite activities...
   - I love to go to...

5. Pass out the *Shield* handouts or have participants do this activity in their journals.

6. Ask participants to fill their shields by creatively exhibiting topics from the list. The topics they are not comfortable promoting should be done on the backs of their shields. Have them use drawings or symbols to make a their own artistic coat of arms that represents who they are. Encourage them to use creatively written words when they have difficulties drawing what they want to express.

7. When the participants have completed the task, ask the following:

   - Was anyone willing to put all ten topics on the front of their shield? Why or why not?
   - Why do you think some people have topics they don't want people to know about? (They believe it's personal and no one's business, they don't want to appear weak, they might get embarrassed, etc.)

- How many of you are willing to share with the rest of the group what you have on the backs of your shields? How about with just one other person?
- Why do people put up "shields" to protect themselves? (Fear of being hurt, fear of rejection, fear of lack of understanding, etc.)
- What enables people to let their "shields" down and let others in a bit? (Feeling safe, knowing they will be accepted for who they are and not be rejected or judged, etc.)

8. Explain that most people construct invisible, protective shields around themselves, especially in unfamiliar situations. This group experience is meant to create an atmosphere where individuals can feel they can let their shields down and feel safe to be themselves. Insist that everyone helps to make the environment one where they can feel free to take risks and open up to others.

9. Have the group come up with a list of what people need in order to let their shields down.

10. Put forth that protective shields tend to grow thicker with each disappointing experience. Ask everyone to be sensitive to their peers' willingness to let their shields down; everyone proceeds at a different pace for different reasons.

11. Discuss with the group how protective shields can be useful in life. They can help people feel safe until they're ready to trust and open up to others. At times we can consciously or unconsciously use shields as coping mechanisms in order to protect ourselves from stressful, painful, or traumatic situations. Explain that this technique of emotional detachment can be unhealthy if used all the time. It can lead to isolation and destroy personal relationships. It's good to have awareness of your protective shield throughout life and to know when and how to use it appropriately.

12. Take some time to let participants share their shields, fronts and backs, as a group or with partners.

*"There came a time when the risk to remain tight in the bud
was more painful than the risk it took to blossom."*

—Anais Nin

smile inside

Interactive Journal

Participants will answer assigned journal questions and engage in an ongoing written dialogue with the facilitator. They will take notes and respond to concepts presented during the course.

materials   journals or paper, pens, a brightly colored pen

1. Post a prompt or question from the list of Journal Entry Topics on the following page each time you meet. Give everyone the first ten minutes of the session to reflect on and respond to it. Choose topics that are relevant to the subject being discussed, current issues, or the planned activity.

2. Encourage participants to write their joys, concerns, successes, and frustrations—anything they care to share with you.

3. Periodically read the journals and then respond with positive comments and questions that will help participants reflect even further. When writing notes in a participant's journal, use a colored pen so your responses can be found easily.

4. Never correct journal writing, especially spelling. Without fear of correction, participants tend to feel free to share more and let their emotions flow through their writing.

5. Encourage participants to individualize their journals artistically.

6. For important information on using journals with your group, see page xiii.

"The reward of a thing well done is to have done it."

—Ralph Waldo Emerson

smile inside

- Last weekend I…
- Describe yourself using more than 100 words.
- Describe your ideal school.
- Draw a map of your bedroom. Describe it in detail. Why do you like it or not like it?
- If you could travel anywhere in the world, where would it be? Why?
- Can you truly be yourself with your friends? Explain what your relationships with them are like.
- What does it mean to accept diversity? How do feel about it?
- If you had to lose one of your senses, which would it be? Why?
- If you could travel to the past or the future, what would you do? Why?
- Who do you admire? What are their positive qualities and what has he or she accomplished?
- What are your favorite things to learn about? How do you learn best?
- Which invention has helped humanity the most? Why?
- Why do you think people dream? Have you ever had a reoccurring or frightening dream? What was it?
- When was the first time you did something forbidden? What happened?
- Have you ever done anything illegal? What happened?
- If you had to be an animal, which one would you choose and why?
- What's your favorite book, movie, or TV show? What is it about?
- What causes you stress? How do you deal with it?
- What are your views on plastic surgery to improve one's looks?
- What would you do if you found out you/your girlfriend were pregnant? Why?
- In what ways would you like to change yourself? Why?
- How are you selfish? How are you selfless?
- What's your opinion of (insert current news)?
- What's your relationship with your family like?
- Why do you think some individuals hurt others physically? Emotionally?
- What would you do if you had one million dollars to spend in one year?
- Describe your ultimate dream house. Draw the floor plan.
- Have you ever had an accident? What happened?
- Make up a word and its definition.
- Do you consider yourself a positive or a negative person? Why?
- Is money power? Why or why not?
- Are you a product of your environment? Explain.
- What do you think it was like to live in the '60s, '70s, '80s, or '90s? How are people different now?
- How do you think society has changed since the year 2000?
- This is what is bottled up inside of me and it really matters:
- Is it easier to die for what you believe in than to live up to what you believe in? Explain.
- Have you made a decision that's had a major impact on your life? How did it change things? What would things be like if you'd chosen differently?
- What were the circumstances surrounding the last time you were compassionate?
- How do you think teenagers manipulate their parents?
- What do you picture yourself doing in ten years?
- What qualities would you want in a lifelong partner? Why are these qualities important to you?
- Do you play mind games with people? How?
- What person has influenced you the most? How?
- Does anyone ever make you feel guilty? How?
- What would you do if your best friend contracted HIV? How do you think your parents would react?
- If you were the leader of your country, what changes would you make to benefit the people?

Why can't people see the real me?

Why?
Why can't people see the real me?
I try so hard to be the perfect person I can be.
Sure I'm young, quiet and shy.
But I'm such an amazing person, which many pass by.
Why?
Why can't people just take the time?
Just tell me your favorite thing to do and I'll tell you mine.
The people that do, I hold dear to my heart.
They see me as mysterious, sweet, funny and smart.
You can't expect me to open up the very first day.
It takes time, but trust me, I'll soon have a lot to say.
Why?
Why can't people wait and get to know the real me?
I bet you I'd be a much different person than you first did see.

—Mantica Mosselli

smile inside

FOCUS & LISTENING

The pace of society has accelerated, and youth are dealing with unrelenting overstimulation from pop culture, technological advances, and the media. In this age of information, there are more choices available than ever before. Vast amounts of helpful, but also time-wasting websites are just a click away. Wading through so much in order to find what you're looking for without becoming distracted takes self-discipline.

The activities in this module give participants the time to experiment with the concepts of being fully present, mastery of mind, and self-control in order to strengthen their abilities to focus.

One of the best ways to learn focus is to practice balancing the body. It's nearly impossible to stand on one leg with one arm in the air without focus. To bring the daydreamers back from the clouds, use *Be a Tree* (p. 14), which offers a selection of grounding balancing postures. *Walk and Talk* (p. 16) has participants walking while listening with a focus on verbal self-control.

During *Where's Your Head At?* (p. 17) and *Mesmerize Me* (p. 19), participants take part in valuable exercises that discipline the mind and provide lifelong benefits. *Wanna Buy a Bunny?* (p. 20) is a fun memory game for practicing focus.

In our daily interactions, the inability to focus on what someone is saying can lead to misunderstandings, mishaps, disappointments, and failure in reaching goals as well as wounded relationships. Many of these troubles and emotional pains could be avoided if people were willing to slow down and really listen to each other. *Active Listening* (p. 21) highlights focusing while listening to a complaint or problem and familiarizes participants with the skills needed to help someone feel valued when speaking.

This module lays the foundation needed for the highest level of success in the activities in this handbook and helps participants increase their capacities for learning in general.

Be a Tree

Participants will strengthen their ability to focus by practicing balancing postures.

materials   *Balancing Postures* handouts, open space with carpet or grass

1. Begin the session by asking the participants to spread out and find their own spots, preferably in an open, carpeted area. This activity works best if participants take their shoes off.

2. Explain that yoga is a physical and mental discipline that helps people learn to calm their minds and focus. Challenge the participants to be fully present within their bodies while attempting the yoga balancing postures.

3. Demonstrate the poses yourself or share the images from the handout. Ask everyone to pay close attention to their weight shifting on the soles of their feet.

4. Do the standing poses first and proceed in order of difficulty: warrior two, warrior three, tree, dancer, table, boat, and crow.

5. Encourage participants to see how long they can hold a pose and then work to increase that time on each trial.

6. Emphasize that this is not a competition, only a personal challenge to test their ability to remain focused.

7. Pass out the *Balancing Postures* handouts so the participants can practice at home.

Balancing Postures

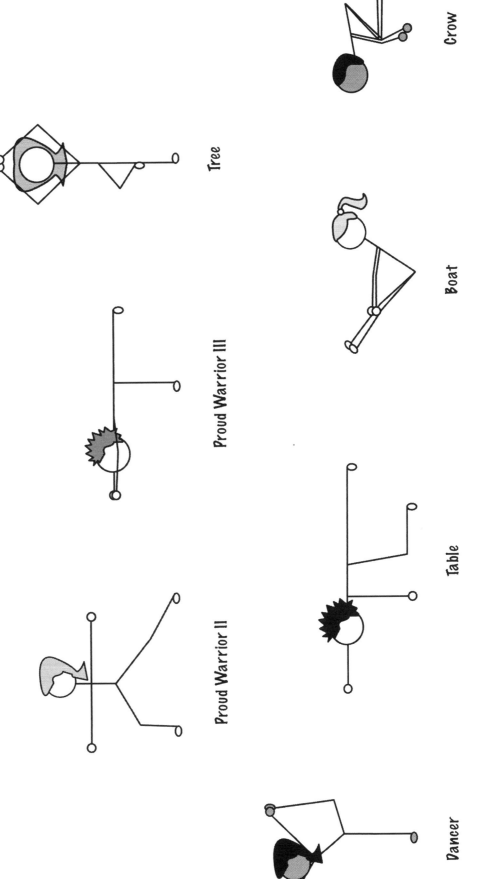

Tree

Crow

Proud Warrior III

Boat

Proud Warrior II

Table

Dancer

smile inside

Walk & Talk

Participants will take turns speaking without being interrupted and practice restraint while listening. They will reflect on their feelings associated with the activity and discuss self-discipline. They will listen and contribute in a conversation without restrictions.

25 min

materials   open area for taking a walk

1. Pair the participants and ask them to decide who will be the first speaker. Explain the boundaries for the walk they will soon take.

2. Explain the *Walk and Talk* rules:

   - While walking with your partners, the speakers must talk until you reach the turnaround point. Talk about anything you wish or just say whatever comes up in your mind.
   - The listeners must not laugh or interrupt, regardless of how much you want to say something.
   - Once you reach the turnaround point (or when time is up) switch roles.

3. As they return, ask the partners:

   - Was it harder to speak or listen?
   - How did you feel after talking for that long?
   - How did it feel when you wanted to say something but could not?

4. After everyone has returned ask the group:

   - What's it called when you have control over your speech? (E.g., restraint, verbal self-control, self-discipline, biting your tongue.)
   - How were you able to stay silent? What was going on in your head?
   - When else might you need to practice some form of self-discipline? (When it's important to be polite and you have nothing nice to say, when dealing with peer pressure, with food, with the television, phone, or Internet, etc.)
   - How can you become more self-disciplined?
   - What did this activity help you realize about your behavior in conversation?

5. Allow the pairs to refresh and conclude their conversations, this time with the freedom of asking the appropriate questions at the appropriate time.

smile inside

Where's Your Head At?

Participants will focus on repeating numbers within their minds. They will organize their thoughts into past, present, and future "files" and then repeat the number challenge.

materials   a watch with a second hand or a silent timer

1. Tell the participants this activity is about increasing the attention span and one's capacity to focus. It also helps develop will power and a stronger mind.

2. Explain the technique:

    > Repeat the number one silently to yourself over and over until something distracts you. If you think about anything besides the number one, even if a sound draws your attention away from the task, you must go to number two. Say, "Two, two, two..." to yourself, focusing all your mind power on the number. If you get distracted, go to number three. If you get distracted again, go to number four and so on. Keep going until I say "stop."

3. Advise that this exercise is easier with the eyes closed. Give the participants a moment to prepare, then cue them to begin. After exactly one minute say "stop."

4. Ask everyone to answer the following questions by raising their hands:

    *   Who was able to remain on number one the entire time?
    *   When I said "stop" who was on number two (three, four, five, six, etc.)?

5. Ask the participants to share what kinds of thoughts or things distracted them.

6. Explain that the goal of this exercise is to improve each time you do it. Let the group know you timed them for exactly sixty seconds. For those who stayed on one the entire time, their goal is to increase the amount of time they can remain on one in the future. Everyone else needs to work on reducing their numbers for the sixty-second period.

7. Explain the next technique in which they will be organizing their random thoughts into past, present, and future boxes within their minds:

    > Now we're going to try something that will help you clear your mind. I want you to observe your mind and your thoughts. You are going to file each thought that comes up into one of three imagined boxes. Take a deep breath and relax. Close your eyes and picture the three boxes. The box on the left has *past* written on it, the box in the middle has *present* written on it, and the box on the right has *future* written on it. If you can't picture the boxes, imagine you're sending the thoughts

away from you in those three directions. Examine what you're thinking. If you're thinking, *I wish (s)he'd stop talking so we can get on with it* or *I'm hungry* then those thoughts would go into the box labeled *present*. If you're thinking about a television show from last night, that goes into the box labeled *past*. If you're thinking about what you might have for a snack when you get home, put that thought into the box labeled *future*. Take some time now to clear your minds by filing away your thoughts.

8. Stop them after a few minutes and explain that now their minds are clear, it should be easier to focus. Repeat the first exercise and ask for a show of hands to see how many were able to increase their attention spans. Discuss.

9. As a variation for musically minded participants, use *do, re, mi, fa, so, la, ti, do* instead of numbers for the internal focus point. As a more challenging option, have participants focus on a color while attempting to keep the mind completely silent.

"Those who mind don't matter, and those who matter don't mind."

—Bernard M. Baruch

smile inside

Mesmerize Me

Participants will regulate their auditory focus. They will discover the influence of distractions on their ability to concentrate and practice dismissing them.

materials   music player, instrumental, popular, and classical music, an excerpt from a nonfiction book

1. Explain that the following exercises will help everyone develop their ability to focus.

2. Play a piece of music with a variety of instruments and ask the group to focus all their attention on just one of the instruments. After about thirty seconds, ask them to switch their focus to another instrument, this time for one minute. Advise them to concentrate even harder for the second round because it is twice as long.

3. Stop the music and ask the group:

   - Who was able to do that easily?
   - Who had difficulty?
   - Do any of you play an instrument? Was it easy or difficult for you to concentrate?
   - Who was able to focus on the first instrument the entire time without being distracted?
   - Who was able to focus on the second instrument the entire time without being distracted?

4. Ask a volunteer to read an excerpt from a nonfiction book aloud to the group. Play some random music at the same volume the volunteer is reading. Challenge the group to focus only on what their peer is reading.

5. Switch the music to a very popular song and then to a piece of classical music. Clap or cough to cause even more distractions.

6. Ask the group:

   - Who can paraphrase what (volunteer's name) has just read aloud to us?
   - Who was most distracted by the (first song, popular song, classical song, clapping, coughing, etc.)?
   - Who couldn't focus on what was being read because of all the distractions?
   - When would a skill of being able to regulate your auditory focus be useful? (When doing homework with background noise, when reading a book on a bus, when listening to someone at an event with music, etc.)
   - How do you believe one can acquire a skill like this? (Practice.)

7. Let the participants know that mastering this skill will benefit them in many different circumstances in the future.

Wanna Buy a Bunny?

Participants will use focus, teamwork, memory, and patience to maintain a spoken pattern.

1. Sitting in a circle, explain that there is a purpose behind this strange activity and they can guess at its conclusion. Begin by turning to the person on your left and guide him or her in participating in the following dialogue:

Facilitator:	You wanna buy a bunny?
Person 1:	A what?
Facilitator:	A bunny!
Person 1:	Does it hop?
Facilitator:	Of course it does!
Person 1:	Then I'll buy it.
Facilitator:	Good.
Person 1:	Good.

2. Person 1, supplying their own item for sale, turns to Person 2. The dialogue should go as follows:

Person 1:	You wanna buy a cat?
Person 2:	A what?
Person 1:	A what? (to Facilitator)
Facilitator:	A bunny!
Person 1:	A cat! (to Person 2)
Person 2:	Does it talk?
Person 1:	Does it hop? (to Facilitator)
Facilitator:	Of course it does!
Person 1:	Of course it does!
Person 2:	Then I'll buy it.
Person 1:	Good.
Person 2:	Good.

3. Person 2 turns to Person 3 and the pattern continues:

Person 2:	You wanna buy a car?
Person 3:	A what?
Person 2:	A what? (to Person 1)
Person 1:	A what? (to Facilitator)
Facilitator:	A bunny!
Person 1:	A cat!
Person 2:	A car!
Person 3:	Does it fly?
Person 2:	Does it talk? (to Person 1)
Person 1:	Does it hop? (to Facilitator)
Facilitator:	Of course it does!
Person 1:	Of course it does!
Person 2:	Of course it does!
Person 3:	Then I'll buy it!
Person 2:	Good.
Person 3:	Good.

4. The questioning will eventually come back to the facilitator and the dialogue will begin to overlap. Challenge everyone to focus on their responses and to keep up the pace.

5. Let participants guess what this activity has helped everyone practice (the ability to focus their attention, listening skills, how to work as a team, drama skills, etc.).

Active Listening

Participants will use attentive and active listening skills in response to someone's problem.

materials   *Active Listening Tips* handouts

1. Ask participants to name the signs of an attentive listener (good eye contact, facing the body toward the speaker, not fiddling with anything, nodding in agreement).

2. Explain they will be taking their focusing/listening skills to a new level in the form of active listening, which comes into play when someone is discussing their (usually negative) feelings. Active listening is helpful when someone is frustrated with a problem in his or her life.

3. Active listening is attentive listening with a few more rules. Distribute the handouts and go over the tips for active listening. Simply put, an active listener recognizes another's feelings in relation to a situation and does not try to fix the problem for the other person.

4. Explain that when responding to someone, it's helpful to remember the following active listening formula: *So you feel (an emotion) when (this thing happens).* E.g., "So you get really frustrated when your sister borrows your clothes without asking."

5. Add that another way to empathize is to recognize the other person's feelings by reflecting their feelings back to them. "That really must have upset you!" or "How frustrating!" or "That sounds awful!" are all statements that demonstrate empathy.

6. Ask everyone to find a partner and to think of a pet peeve or a problem. Allow a few minutes for the first speaker to explain in detail what is annoying or frustrating them, providing examples. The active listener should respond, being mindful of the tips for active listening and using the formula provided as a template for a response.

7. Ask a few sets of partners to share the pet peeves or problems that were expressed and the responses they used during the practice period.

8. Ask the group:

   - Who felt their partner really understood their problem? What did they do or say?
   - Who found it difficult to avoid doing something in the Do Not list? What did you do?
   - How did you help the speaker solve their problem without solving it for him or her?
   - Why do you think it's important for people to be able to solve their own problems? (So they can develop the skill; so they don't end up relying on others all the time to solve their problems; because you may not know the whole situation therefore may not be able to give the best advice.)
   - If someone is really confused about what they should do, would it be okay to give them some options to explore? (Yes.) How is this better than telling them what they should do? (They still have to think for themselves and decide what's best for them.)

9. Have the partners switch roles and repeat the process. After time is up, ask if anyone would like to share.

smile inside

Active Listening Tips

Do

- Be concerned

- Make the speaker feel heard and understood

- Recognize his or her feelings

- Make observations

- Ask open-ended questions

- Encourage him or her to make steps to solve the problem

Do Not

- Sound rehearsed

- Solve the problem for the person

- Turn it into a gossip session

- Agree if you feel differently

- Be judgmental

- Tell him or her what to do

- Change the subject

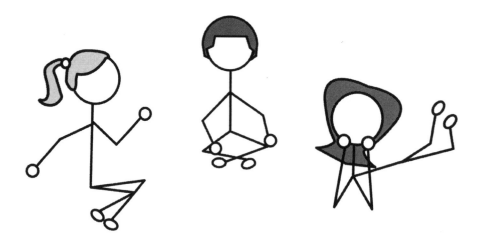

The active listening formula:

*"So you feel (an emotion)
when (this thing happens)."*

Please Listen

When I ask you to listen to me and you start giving me advice,
you have not done what I asked.

When I ask you to listen to me and you begin to tell me why
I shouldn't feel that way, you are trampling on my feelings.

When I ask you to listen to me and you feel you have to do something
to solve my problem, you have failed me, strange as that may seem.

Listen! All I ask is that you listen. Don't talk or do – just hear me.

Advice is cheap; 20 cents will get you both Dear Abby and Billy
Graham in the same newspaper. And I can do for myself; I am not
helpless. Maybe discouraged and faltering, but not helpless.

When you do something for me that I can and need to do for myself,
you contribute to my fear and inadequacy. But when you accept as
a simple fact that I feel what I feel, no matter how irrational, then
I can stop trying to convince you and get about this business
of understanding what's behind this irrational feeling.

And when that's clear, the answers are obvious and I don't need advice.
Irrational feelings make sense when we understand what's behind them.

Perhaps that's why prayer works, sometimes, for some people – because
God is mute, and he doesn't give advice or try to fix things.
God just listens and lets you work it out for yourself.

So please listen, and just hear me. And if you want to talk,
wait a minute for your turn – and I will listen to you.

Author Unknown

smile inside

EMPATHY & RESPECT

Every learning atmosphere must have regulations and a shared understanding to be conducive to productivity, especially when it comes to personal development. Individuals are more likely to take emotional risks if they are in a safe environment where they feel respected and are unconditionally accepted for who they are. This is the space one needs to be in for personal growth to occur.

Laying a foundation for a nonjudgmental and positive atmosphere is done most effectively without the facilitator laying down the rules. A group is more likely to live by a set of rules they create, as in *Right Your Rules* (p. 26). Allowing the group ownership of their environment is the first step toward instilling trust and empathy. It also opens up the participants' understanding of a facilitator's duty to discipline when rules are broken. They need to understand it's about rights, not restrictions.

Individuals can further develop empathy through the activities *Pick Your Perspective* (p. 28), and *The Problem With Villains* (p. 30), which both explore points of view, the feelings of targets, and the motivations behind bullying. The expectation for young people who have developed empathy is that they will think twice when an opportunity to be cruel presents itself. Instead they will be inclusive of others, not tolerate bullying of anyone, and have a new understanding of the behavior of others. *What Happened?* (p. 33) has participants building on their active listening skills as their partners share stories of when they have been treated poorly. Individuals benefit emotionally when others help them feel truly understood. Setting aside this time demonstrates that everyone deserves to feel respected and be supported.

Right Your Rules

Participants will act as council members for an imaginary island country. They will present their ideas about human rights, laws, and consequences for the imaginary island. They will suggest rules and consequences for the group and decide upon the final list. They will write and sign contractual agreements in regard to these rules and consequences.

60 - 90 min

materials   a large sheet of paper for each group, markers, a visual aid, journals or paper, pens

1. Ask for the definition of human rights: things humans deserve or are entitled to, certain freedoms or privileges.

2. Ask for examples of human rights: (e.g., to live, to clean water, to learn, to have the freedom to believe in what one chooses, to have a home, to have a family, to be safe).

3. Have participants form groups of three or four. Tell each group it has been allocated an island and is the presiding council for the island. In twenty minutes, each group needs to come up with the following on a large sheet of paper:

    * A name for the island.
    * A map sketch of what they want the island to look like and what will be on it.
    * Its size and maximum population.

    In addition, each group must answer the following questions:

    * What rights will the people of your island have?
    * What laws need to be created to support the rights of the people?
    * What will the consequences be for people who do not follow the laws?
    * What will happen to people who repeatedly break the laws?

4. Allow each group a few minutes to present its island to the rest of the group. Put the finished products on display.

5. Ask the participants:

    * Why are there laws and rules? (Laws and rules are not just about having order; they're about protecting the rights of individuals.)
    * Do you think it's fair that people lose their rights if they violate a law? Why or why not?
    * Do you think it's reasonable to expect people to have respect for all others at all times? When do you think it's not reasonable?
    * Do you think it's reasonable to expect people to refrain from harming others in all circumstances? When do you think it's not reasonable?
    * What do you think is the key to effective discipline of people who disregard the rights of other people? (Relevant and consistent consequences help.)

6. Brainstorm a list of rules together that will protect their right to learn and feel safe during their time together. Write all suggestions on the visual aid (listen, no insults, don't interrupt, etc.).

7. Draw the group's attention to the fact that every rule falls into one of two categories: having respect or having self-control. Ask them to identify which rules come under which category and label each rule with R or S. If a rule doesn't seem to fall under either of these categories, ask the group to analyze and classify that rule further.

8. Use respect and self-control as the group's code of conduct or compile a list of the ones they want to adopt.

9. Now ask the group to come up with consequences for those who have difficulty respecting others or having self-control during their time together. Get their opinions on whether or not the consequences should be more severe for repeat offenses. List their suggestions on the visual aid and decide together on a final list.

10. Have the group write the adopted rules and consequences in their journals. Have them write the following contractual statement:

> *I agree to abide by these sensible rules. If I do not for whatever reason, I will serve the consequence with a good attitude as a reminder to myself that people have rights and I disregarded their rights.*
>
> X _____ (Signature)
>
> X _____ (Signature of a witness)

11. Alternatively, write the rights, responsibilities, consequences, and the above statement (using *we* instead of *I*) on a poster and have everyone sign it. Display the poster as a reminder of what the group decided together.

"Respect yourself and others will respect you."

—Confucius

Pick Your Perspective

Participants will perceive different points of view in a movie in order to analyze and answer questions about feelings and motivations.

materials   a movie or documentary that portrays some level of bullying (e.g., *Odd Girl Out* [2005], *The Karate Kid* [1984 or 2010], *The New World* [2005], or *The Trials of Phoebe Prince* [2011]), AV equipment, journals or paper, pens

1. Begin watching the movie or documentary, taking note of the main characters as they are introduced.

2. After the main characters have been introduced, pause the movie and ask each member of the group to pick someone he or she would like to follow for the remainder of the movie.

3. Ask the participants to relate to their characters' perspectives in order to justify their actions to the group. Participants can form small groups to observe main or secondary characters in the movie as well. If viewing the documentary *The Trials of Phoebe Prince*, form only three groups: bullies, targets, and bystanders.

4. Advise the participants to take notes on their characters throughout the movie and to be prepared for questions after the movie ends.

5. Continue watching the movie. If a new character is introduced later, ask for volunteers to study the new character's perspective along with their original characters.

6. After the movie, hold a group discussion. When asking the following questions, keep in mind that bullies can also be targets and targets can turn into bullies.

   Questions for those observing a bully:

   - What kinds of emotions did the bully experience?
   - How did his or her emotions and actions affect the outcome of (insert situation)?
   - Why do you think the bully acted the way he or she did when _____?
   - What was the underlying reason behind his or her behavior?
   - How do you think the emotions of the target affected the bully?
   - How could the bully have minimized his or her problems by handling things differently?
   - How would you have done things differently if you were in the bully's position?

   Questions for those observing a target:

   - What do you think the target was going through emotionally when (insert bullying situation)?
   - What do you think about how he or she dealt with the bully?
   - What do you think would have happened if the target _____ instead of _____?
   - How could the target have minimized his or her problems by handling things differently?
   - How would you have handled things differently if you were in the target's position?

Questions for those observing a secondary character:

- How did the bully's actions affect the secondary character?
- Why do you think the secondary character behaved the way he or she did?
- What do you think the secondary character was feeling when the target was being bullied?
- If the secondary character was more (or less) protective of the target what do you think would have happened?
- How would you have done things differently if you were in their position?

General questions:

- Which characters acted from selfish standpoints?
- Which characters acted from selfless standpoints?
- What consequences did the characters pay for their actions? Do you think the consequences were reasonable?
- What consequences do you think the bully/bullies deserved?
- Have you ever heard the saying "what goes around, comes around"? How are consequences related to this saying?
- What is your opinion of karma?
- Did the characters learn any lessons? What were they?
- Do you think it was necessary for any of them to go through that entire experience to learn a lesson?
- Do you find it's necessary to experience something, even if it's painful, to understand it fully?
- Have you heard of the saying "an eye for an eye"? Do you believe others should have to experience the same suffering they cause others?

7. Conclude the discussion by asking what message the movie or documentary gave to them. What did they learn? How did it inspire or motivate them and in what way?

8. Encourage them to journal their feelings and what they want to remember the next time they encounter bullying.

"Resolve to be tender with the young,
compassionate with the aged,
sympathetic with the striving,
and tolerant of the weak and the wrong.
Sometime in life, you will have been all of these."

—Dr. Robert H. Goddard

The Problem With Villains

Participants will provide examples of bullying, analyze the motivation of bullies, and identify the places bullying may occur. They will offer suggestions on how the cycle of hurting in society can be stopped. They will discuss what an atmosphere of safety requires and how bullies are handled in society.

60 - 90 min

materials   a visual aid, journals or paper, pens

1. Ask the group to come up with some well-known villains and to give examples of their behaviors.

2. Ask the group to name the three main kinds of bullying (physical, verbal, and silent/passive/indirect) and put these in columns on the visual aid.

3. Encourage the group members to name different types of bullying they have experienced, witnessed, or seen in the news or on reality television shows. Write their answers in the appropriate columns.

Physical	Verbal	Silent/Passive /Indirect
Violence	Threats	Exclusion
Aggression	Belittlement	Texting
Theft	Intimidation	Gossip
Vandalism	Harassment	Cyber
Sabotage	Teasing	Looks

4. Ask the group:

- So what is the problem with villains?
- What is their motivation? (Getting even, getting ahead, money, fame, seeing others in pain to make themselves feel better, etc.)
- What are their issues?

  ◦ In *Despicable Me*, Gru's motivation to be a famous criminal came from a lack of acknowledgment and love as a child.
  ◦ In *The Simpsons*, Nelson the bully grew up in poverty without a dad and had a poor role model for a mother.
  ◦ In the *Star Wars* episodes, Darth Vader turned to the dark side so he could learn how to save the one he loved, although there were contributing factors: he grew up a slave not knowing his father; his mother was brutalized by a tribe of raiders; he returned to save her but she died in his arms.
  ◦ In the *Harry Potter* series, Voldemort was a self-hating bully who took his anger out on others because he was only a half-blood. He was also afraid of death.

5. Ask, "As for real-life bullies, why do they do it? Why don't they have respect for others?" Get the group to think about the reasons behind the behaviors. Give an example of what an answer might be to begin the brainstorm session. Possible answers:

- Some are competing for alpha positions in their friendship group.
- Some want to satisfy their desires so badly they don't care who they hurt along the way.
- Some are self-centered and have no regard for others' feelings.
- Some believe getting revenge will make them feel better.
- Some think they are serving justice.
- Some do it because it makes them feel superior or powerful when they are really just insecure.
- Some are on the offensive because they have been hurt before and think they can avoid getting hurt again by attacking others first.
- Some like to stay in control of situations.
- Some find it gets them attention, either through people watching them or the consequences it brings.
- Some are imitating what they have seen.
- Some like to rebel against authority because they have anger at another authority figure in their life.
- Some have a lack of awareness of their own behavior and don't know what it is to have empathy for others.
- Some people's behaviors change when they are using addictive substances.
- Some have anger and don't know how to manage it appropriately.

6. Ask, "Where does bullying take place?" Possible answers:

- In homes
- At school
- In the workplace
- In the community
- Online
- In prisons
- Globally, between countries
- Anywhere

7. Ask the participants to form groups for each sector of society that was named. Inform the groups that their task is to brainstorm solutions and present their ideas however they would like, but they must address all of the following questions in their journals:

- How do you believe this cycle of hurting can stop within (families, schools, the workplace, etc.)?
- What should be done to help the targets?
- What should be done to help the bullies?
- Whose responsibility is it to protect the targets and rehabilitate the bullies? Why?
- What is your opinion on those who witness bullying/abuse but do nothing to help the targets?
- What top solution would you offer to those responsible for stopping this cycle of hurting?

8. Give the groups about fifteen minutes to answer the questions and discuss solutions. Ask each group to present its ideas to the rest of the groups.

9. Further questions for discussion:

- Do you think punishing bullies works? Why or why not?
- What consequences do you think would be the most effective to get bullies to stop hurting others?
- What kind of atmosphere needs to exist in order for people to feel they are safe and can truly be themselves? (One that offers acceptance, trust, respect, etc.)

- What kinds of behaviors cannot be present in an atmosphere of safety? (Discrimination, disrespect of another's feelings, non-acceptance, judgmental attitudes, nastiness, etc.)
- Do you think all people deserve to be treated with respect? Why or why not?
- In what situations may there be an atmosphere of disrespect, but it might be outside of one's control to change it? (In a prison; in politics; at home; in the military, when superiors are training or disciplining troops, etc.)
- How do you think disrespectful attitudes and behaviors can be discouraged?
- Do you know about anything that is being done to address bullying?

10. Compile a list of tips and strategies to deal with bullies. Start with the following:

- When someone's attitude and behavior starts to affect you, stand up for yourself. Tell them you don't like it.
- Even though someone's offensive actions are not under your control, remember that you do have control over your reactions to their behavior.
- You may not be able to change others, but you can encourage them to seek help or find a way for them to help themselves.
- Inspire others by being the best person you can be.

11. Remind the participants that during their time together, an atmosphere of respect, acceptance, trust, and safety must prevail. This allows everyone to feel comfortable enough to dissolve the protective shields they put up and just be themselves.

"No one can make you feel inferior without your consent."

—Eleanor Roosevelt

smile inside

What Happened?

Participants will share personal experiences of being bullied. They will practice empathy using active listening skills. They will show others they are valued.

1. Have participants find partners they do not know very well.

2. Remind participants of the active listening tips and formula (p. 22). Explain they will need to use the past tense version of the formula in this activity: *So you must have felt (an emotion) when (that thing happened)* or *That must have been (adjective) when (that thing happened).*

3. Ask everyone to find a comfortable place to sit and take turns talking about their own experiences of being bullied, or mistreated by someone close to them. Encourage the partners to empathize with each other by asking themselves, "How would that have felt?"

4. Ask the partners to discuss why that person may have lashed out or treated them poorly.

5. Share with the group that when someone is "knocked down," it takes longer for them to "get back up." Discuss how one put-down can be alleviated by three put-ups.

6. Tell them their assignment is to do three nice things for their partner in the next week. Encourage them to be as creative as they want (send them a nice note, bake them cookies, deliver a surprise package, give them a compliment, etc.).

7. Insist that if anyone has discovered someone is being bullied at present they report it immediately.

8. After one week, follow up by asking the participants to share what their partners did.

*"There is no greater agony
than bearing an untold story inside you."*

—Maya Angelou

smile inside

SELF-TALK

Self-talk is our inner dialogue, giving an ongoing commentary on our self-image, our actions, and our life in general. The self-talk of an optimistic person is positive and supportive, but many others experience self-talk as negative and self-defeating. This internal chatter can become quite the nuisance and detrimental if not managed properly.

There is also the famous angel versus devil metaphor that represents our conscience. Richard Bach writes, "Your conscience is the measure of the honesty of your selfishness." We can be of great service to our personal growth if we can become the masters of our self-talk and not servants to it.

Acknowledging how our thought processes affect us and perpetuate the beliefs we hold about ourselves is a positive step toward developing self-awareness. With these new insights comes the choice to work toward mastering the mind, which will provide a definite advantage in life.

Who Are You? (p. 36) challenges participants to examine what their self-talk says about their self-images. They contemplate what can happen with an untamed mind and consider self-discipline in *Who Decides the Ride?* (p. 39). Finally participants put their inner selves on display in *Self-Study Collage* (p. 42).

These activities empower the participants and prepare them for the process of self-discovery in the next module, Self-Exploration.

Who Are You?

Participants will listen to and share their self-talk about their self-image. They will analyze their self-talk by categorizing their responses into roles, qualities, and other concepts. They will discuss the impermanence of change.

45 min

materials *Who Are You?* handouts, *Analysis of Who Are You?* handouts, journals or paper, pens

1. Ask the participants to find partners. Explain this activity is about listening to one's self-talk in response to a single question. Encourage the participants to clear their minds and become acutely aware of their reactive thoughts.

2. Pass out the *Who Are You?* handouts. Have the pairs interview each other, asking, "Who are you?" back and forth and writing down their partners' replies. The process should continue until they each have thirty different and honest responses. It is best to allow the pairs to spread out and sit where they would like to limit distractions during the interview. Another option would be to suggest that participants write their responses independently for the second column on the handout.

3. Require the following: all participants, using their partners' notes, should write *R* next to the responses they consider roles, *Q* next to the responses they consider qualities, and circle the ones they feel do not fit into these two categories. Some examples:

   • Roles: me, daughter/son, friend, student, worker, singer, soccer player, volunteer.
   • Qualities: nice, friendly, lazy, funny, smart, interesting, fair, loving, warm, shy, nervous.
   • Other: a leader who will change the world, Superman, ready to go home, tired, needing love, brunette, who I am.

4. Ask participants to put a plus sign next to positive responses and a minus sign next to negative responses.

5. Pass out the *Analysis of Who Are You?* handouts for the participants to complete. Discuss.

6. Have the participants write their first and/or last names vertically in their journals. Have them match some of their positive responses with the letters of their names. For example:

Loveable

Interesting

Lucky

Youth Leader

smile inside

Who Are You?

smile inside

I am	I am
I am	I am
I am	I am
I am	I am
I am	I am
I am	I am
I am	I am
I am	I am
I am	I am
I am	I am
I am	I am
I am	I am
I am	I am

"Today you are you, that is truer than true.
There is no one alive that is you-er than you."

— Dr. Seuss

smile inside

Analysis of Who Are You?

How many of your responses were roles? (E.g. friend, student, son/daughter, etc.)

How many of your responses were qualities? (E.g. friendly, lazy, smart, funny, etc.)

What categories could you create to fit some of your other responses into?
(E.g. feelings, appearance, needs, etc.)

How many items on your list are positive?

How many items on your list are negative?

Are you more optimistic or pessimistic in the way you think about yourself?

Could any category be considered permanent, something that will never change?

What do you think about the following quote by Henri Bergson: "To exist is to change, to change is to mature, to mature is to go on creating oneself endlessly"?

Do you believe any part of you remains the same forever? Why or why not?

What did this activity teach you about yourself?

smile inside

Who Decides the Ride?

Participants will record their self-talk. They will examine a metaphor for an undisciplined mind and identify what distracts them from their goals. They will offer solutions for self-control and visualize themselves in the future with self-discipline.

materials   journals or paper, pens, *Who Decides the Ride?* handouts

1. Explain that this activity is about recording their thoughts. Ask everyone to write every single thing they hear in their minds for three minutes. Emphasize the importance of being completely honest in observing what is going on inside their heads. State that this exercise is private and they will not have to share aloud what they have written if they do not want to. Tell them to write "nothing" during the time they do not observe any thoughts. They should be writing the entire three minutes.

2. When time is up, participants should have about a page of written thoughts. Extend the time of the exercise if they have difficulty getting started. Ask for volunteers to read their thought recordings aloud.

3. Ask the group:

   o Does anyone know what this type of talk in the mind has been called? (E.g., self-talk, intrapersonal communication, stream of consciousness, inner voice, mental chatter, inner dialogue, internal monologue, internal speech)
   o Does anyone feel as though their thoughts seem to go really fast at times?
   o Does anyone feel as though they have full control over what is going on in their mind? (If yes, how do you manage to keep your thoughts under control?)
   o Is there anyone who can maintain absolute silence within their mind? For how long?

4. Explain that you are going to share a metaphor with everyone that will help them understand their self-talk. Pass out the *Who Decides the Ride?* handouts. Ask participants to answer the first question.

5. Discuss the parts of the horse and cart metaphor. Point out that the driver's job is to obey the passenger's command by driving the horses to the destination.

   o Cart = your body
   o Passenger = your intelligence
   o Driver = your mind
   o Tame horses = your self-discipline
   o Wild horses = distractions, uncontrolled desires, addictions

6. Explain the metaphor further:

   o The cart represents our body and is how we get around in life.
   o The passenger, our intelligence, knows what's best for us and tells the driver, our mind, where to go.
   o If the driver hasn't trained the horses properly, the cart will be pulled off track and steer us away from our goals.

7. Explain that the mind attempts to steer us in the right direction in life by making the right decisions but distractions, uncontrolled desires, and addictions can make it difficult to attain our goals. Self-discipline is when the mind and the intelligence are working as a team and is the key to reaching our goals successfully.

8. Ask the group:

   - What could a short-term destination for a passenger be? (Be home on time.) Long-term? (Good grades in school.)
   - What could an out of control, wild horse represent? (Harmful or time-wasting behaviors/habits like: excessive video game playing, talking on the phone too much, watching too much TV, overeating, etc.)
   - What's the metaphor for the horses dragging the cart off track across a field? (Getting distracted.)
   - Do you think it's possible for someone to lose their way altogether (lose sight of their goal) if their horses are wild? How?
   - How does someone stop the horses from recklessly dragging the cart all over the place? (The horses need to be tamed through self-discipline.)
   - What happens to people who do things in excess with no discipline? Ask yourself, "Do I live to eat or eat to live?" How much time do you waste when you should be doing research online for school?
   - Do you have any wild horses? What uncontrolled desires/habits/behaviors would you like to tame?

9. Ask the participants to complete the handouts.

10. Have the participants form groups of three or four and answer the following question: "How can wild horses be tamed?"

11. After they have had time to discuss the question, ask each group to impart their best ideas. Possible answers/discussion points include:

    - Take up a hobby that requires self-discipline like martial arts, yoga, music, or running.
    - Practice self-control through will power.
    - Win small battles in your mind first, then up the ante each time.
    - Set targets for learning to control your mind.
    - Practice focusing for longer and longer periods.
    - Visualize your future goals often.
    - Remind yourself to stay on track by posting your goals where you can see them every day.
    - Bad habits can hold you back. Don't add them to your life—subtract them.
    - Make sure the driver is not asleep at the wheel. If so, wake him or her up!
    - Make deals with yourself using positive or negative reinforcement.

12. To conclude, ask participants to close their eyes and think about when their wildest horse is most out of control. Ask them to picture themselves in the future without that bad habit holding them back. Have them ask themselves, "What am I doing differently?" Challenge them to put this plan into action so that it is them who is deciding their ride, not the wild horses.

smile inside

Who Decides the Ride?

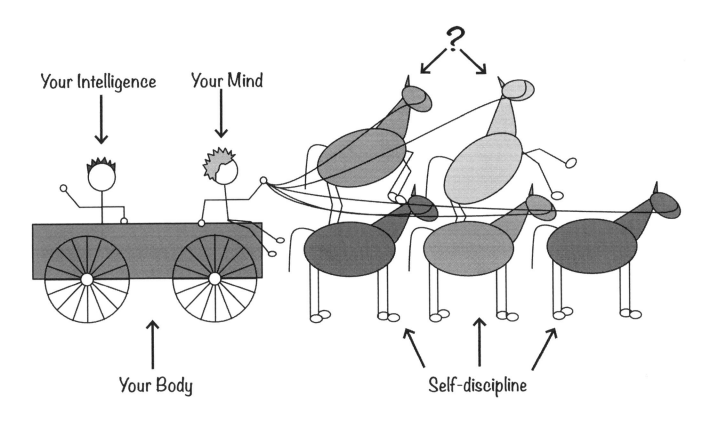

Your Intelligence

Your Mind

?

Your Body

Self-discipline

In the image above, if the tame horses symbolize self-discipline, what do the wild horses represent?

Name two of your most *wild horses* :

What is something you really want to achieve?

How do your *wild horses* try to stop you from getting there?

How might someone tame a *wild horse* ?

What can you do to make sure a *wild horse* doesn't stop you from reaching a goal?

smile inside

Self-Study Collage

Participants will make collages that represent who they are.

90 min

materials *Self-Study Collage* handouts, Internet and printer access and/or magazines and newspapers to be cut up, scissors, glue sticks, poster board or construction paper, a laminator

1. A few days before the activity is to take place, distribute the *Self-Study Collage* handouts. Encourage the participants to bring in magazines to be cut up.

2. For durability, use poster board, otherwise use construction paper and laminate the finished products.

3. On collage-making day, lightly monitor while everyone creates their personal artwork. Invite participants to listen to their self-talk in order to portray honest depictions of their self-image and innermost thoughts and feelings.

4. Each participant's collage can be shared with the group when he or she gives his or her *ME-Day* presentation (p. 74) or after everyone has finished making their collages. Ask everyone to be prepared to explain why they chose certain pictures or phrases to describe themselves.

*"Before you make the most of what you have,
you have to realize what it is.
Before you decide how you want to live your life,
you must look at yourself and attempt to know yourself."*

—Don Schollander

Self-Study Collage

You're going to put together a piece of art: a self-study in a collage format. It will consist of many pictures and a few words or phrases that portray who you are. The pictures may represent your likes and favorites in areas like food, clothes, movies, sports, heroes, activities, emotions, goals, and values. You may choose whatever appeals to you in any way. It will be a visual description of your inner self and something you may want to keep for a long time.

A good collage is so full of images that none of the background shows in between the pictures and words. They are cut, overlapped, and situated so an observer must keep turning the collage around to see everything. When finished examining it, one has a pretty good idea what the artist is like.

Start collecting pictures and words from magazines and newspapers that speak your truth. Print images from the Internet that represent you. You may also want to draw pictures or words that can be placed on the collage.

"The real voyage of discovery consists not in seeking new landscapes but in having new eyes."

–Marcel Proust

smile inside

SELF-EXPLORATION

Personal development is an ongoing journey for anyone who chooses to invest in themselves. It can also be a very delicate process and needs to be carried out in a reflective and gentle manner. When young people are presented with the occasion to enhance their self-awareness and the tools to facilitate their personal growth, they are more likely to engage in the process throughout their lives. When life's demands begin to limit their progress, one of the activities in this module may inspire them to get back on the right track in the future.

Youth deserve the opportunity to contemplate their feelings about their needs, values, and authenticity. If done in an atmosphere of mutual respect, it will assist them in developing a stronger connection with their genuine selves.

Timeline (p. 46) and *Knowing My Needs* (p. 51) require the analysis of physical, social, and emotional needs. Participants will discover what is truly important to them by examining their choices in *An Auction of Values* (p. 57) and *The Power of Choice* (p. 60). They will then reflect on their prioritized values and choices in hindsight during *Auction Analysis* (p. 62). Evaluating their thoughts, feelings, and actions in all these activities helps the participants comprehend their behaviors and motivations.

Participants look more deeply at the concepts of feelings and self through introspective poems and the creative process in *Please Hear That I Am Me* (p. 67). Becoming more familiar with internal processes will reaffirm their convictions as they give their presentations on themselves on their *ME Day* (p. 74).

Timeline

Participants will keep track of their use of time and diets for one week.
They will analyze their data and answer questions concerning the results.
They will identify improvements they would like to make in
their diets and in their management of time.

2 x 3 days
+2 x 30 min

materials   *Timeline and Food Diary* handouts (six for each participant), *Timeline and Food Diary Analyses* handouts (two for each participant), *Timeline and Food Diary Reflection* handouts, *Time Tips* handouts, journals, or paper, pens, a visual aid

1. Explain to the participants that they will keep a record of their daily activities and food intake for three days. The results will be analyzed and then they will record for another three days.

2. Pass out the *Timeline and Food Diary* handouts three days to one week before the first analysis day. They may prefer to use a pocket notebook to collect their data instead of the handouts.

3. Instruct participants to record the activity they are doing for each hour of the day. Ask them to try to keep their descriptions to one or two words such as sleeping, eating, school, exercising, watching TV, going online, studying, talking, and so on. Every meal should be accounted for as well, including the quantity and types of food and drink consumed.

4. After the participants have collected data for three days, pass out the *Analyses* and *Reflection* handouts. Ask them to analyze and reflect on their use of time and diet.

5. Ask the participants to identify a habit they may be able to adjust or eliminate to improve the way in which they manage their time. Ask them to identify one improvement they would like to make in their diets.

6. Pass out the *Time Tips* handouts. Discuss the tips with the group and ask if anyone has any they would like to add.

7. Challenge participants to keep track of their activities and diets for three more days.

8. At the end of the three days, pass out the second *Analyses* handouts. Ask participants to analyze their new data and compare the differences.

9. Have participants write one last reflection on this exercise in their journals.

Food Diary

Breakfast

Snack

Lunch

Snack

Dinner

Name: _____

smile inside

Timeline

1am

2am

3am

4am

5am

6am

7am

8am

9am

10am

11am

12 noon

1pm

2pm

3pm

4pm

5pm

6pm

7pm

8pm

9pm

10pm

11pm

12 midnight

Date: _____

47

Timeline & Food Diary Analyses

Show how your time was spent on a bar graph:

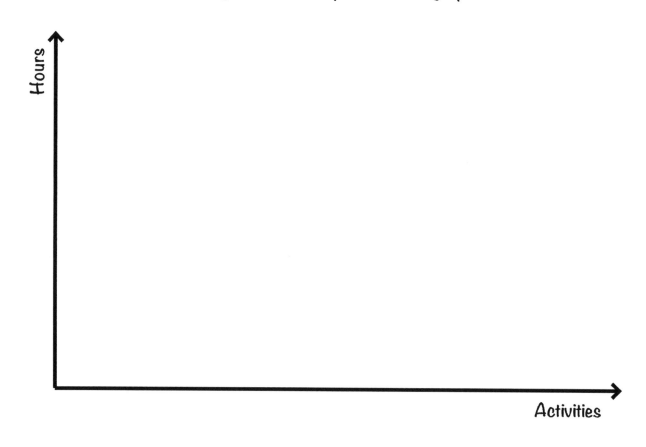

Hours

Activities

Tally your food intake under the following categories:

Fruit and Vegetables	Dairy	Grains and Carbohydrates	Protein	Junk

Timeline & Food Diary Reflection

Rank your activities according to hours spent.

What was the average amount of hours you spent sleeping each night?

What activity did you do the most, excluding sleeping and school?

How much time did you spend exercising?

What time did you go to bed each night? Wake up each morning?

How much time did you spend doing homework?

What activity did you most enjoy during the week? The least?

What activity would you like to do more often? Less often?

Compare your list of fruits and vegetables to your list of junk food.

Which activities took place after your largest meals?

What types of meat did you eat?

From which animal did you have the most meat?

How long did you typically fast each night?

smile inside

Time Tips

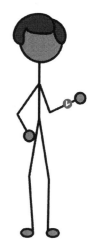

BE ORGANIZED!

- To-do lists really work.
- Make your to-do list in a planner.
- Break large tasks into smaller tasks.
- Prioritize the things that have to be done.

BE EFFICIENT!

- Deal with things immediately if possible.
- Avoid procrastination.
- Eliminate or reduce time-wasting habits.
- Set boundaries with people who waste your time.
- Learn how to say "no" nicely, without guilt.

BE HEALTHY!

- Remember that your energy levels and ability to be productive are directly related to what you put into your body and how well you sleep.
- Be consistent with good habits that support your health.
- Schedule activities that will benefit your well-being.

"We are what we repeatedly do.
Excellence, then, is not an act but a habit."

-Aristotle

smile inside

Knowing My Needs

Participants will analyze in writing how their needs have and have not been met using Maslow's Hierarchy of Needs. They will discuss in writing their views on what it means to be a self-actualized person.

materials   a visual aid, *Hierarchy of Needs* handouts, *Needs Analysis* handouts or journals, pens

1. Introduce Abraham Maslow to the group. He studied human behavior and presented his findings in 1943 in a paper called *A Theory of Human Motivation*. Inform the group that there are other theories about motivation, but for the purpose of this activity Maslow's Hierarchy of Needs will be used as a framework for discussion about human needs and behavior.

2. Draw a large triangle with five tiers on the visual aid. Write the categories of needs (physical, safety, love, and self-respect) working from the base to the top. Ask the participants to come up with examples of each of the needs. Write self-actualization at the top and then convey the following:

   > To be able to fulfill one's unique potential is called self-actualization, according to Abraham Maslow. He states that in order to reach self-actualization, there are needs that have to be met. These include physical needs such as food, clothing, and shelter; also a feeling of safety, both physical and financial. He states that one needs to feel love and affection by belonging to a caring family or group of some sort. Finally, he believes one must have self-respect—the desire to feel proud because of one's achievements. Maslow theorizes that most people must have this base of needs met as a prerequisite for self-actualization.

3. Pass out the *Hierarchy of Needs* handouts. Discuss how a person can be affected when their needs are unsatisfied or imbalanced.

   Physical (physiological)

   - These are the most basic of all needs. They include breathing, sleeping, eating, drinking water, urinating, excreting, and having warmth.
   - Unsatisfied physical needs leave one dwelling on what the body is lacking. It is difficult to focus on anything else. Not having these needs met can be overwhelming and can cause people to feel sickness, pain, and discomfort.

   Safety (security)

   - This need is about feeling safe and secure. People want to feel they are safe from harm. This can include a feeling of financial security, having a steady job, or knowing someone is looking after them.
   - An unsatisfied safety need brings negative emotions of worry, doubt, and fear.

Love (social)

- This need involves relationships, acceptance, and affection. It also includes the desire to feel like one belongs to a group of some sort. Some people never move beyond this point. They get so involved with satisfying their love need they don't have the time or see the value in gaining self-respect or self-actualization.
- An unsatisfied love need can cause possessiveness and an inability to love appropriately as an adult. Not having this need met brings loneliness, social anxiety, and depression.

Self-Respect (self-esteem)

- This is an internal feeling of worth and confidence in one's abilities. It is about having some degree of success in something. Many need to feel they have contributed to the world. Others may need recognition or approval or feel they have secured a position of status. This need includes the desire to be respected by others. With self-respect comes the expectation that one should be treated well by others.
- A lack of self-respect leads people to believe they are worthless and unable to accomplish anything meaningful. Imbalances in this area can cause inferiority complexes, an inflated sense of self-importance, and snobbishness.

Self-Actualization

- Self-actualized people are creative and spontaneous in their ideas and actions. They embrace things in the world with appreciation but can still see things logically and objectively. They have strong values and morals and a gift for solving problems. A person who reaches this state finds happiness and peace in bringing joy to others. Simply put, it is about realizing one's fullest potential.
- Those who do not attain this level of self-realization may seem self-centered or apathetic. They have prejudices and lack a strong set of values and morals. They do not strive for personal growth or creative expression.

4. Ask, "Do you believe all these needs have to be met in order to become self-actualized?" Discuss.

5. Pass out the *Needs Analysis* handouts. Ask participants to complete the analyses during the session or at home on the handouts or in their journals. Once it's collected, respond to their entries as soon as possible.

"The most important human endeavor is the striving for morality in our actions. Our inner balance and even our very existence depend on it. Only morality in our actions can give beauty and dignity to life."

—Charles Dickens

smile inside

Self-Respect

This is an internal feeling of worth and confidence in one's abilities. It is about having some degree of success in something. Many need to feel they have contributed to the world. Others may need recognition or approval or feel they have secured a position of status. This need includes the desire to be respected by others. With self-respect comes the expectation that one should be treated well by others.

Unsatisfied or Imbalanced:

A lack of self-respect leads people to believe they are worthless and unable to accomplish anything meaningful. Imbalances in this area can cause an inflated sense of self-importance, an inferiority complexes, and snobbishness.

Love

This need involves relationships, acceptance, and affection. It also includes the desire to feel like one belongs to a group of some sort. Some people never move beyond this point. They get so involved with satisfying their love need they don't have the time or see the value in gaining self-respect or self-actualization.

Unsatisfied or Imbalanced:

An unsatisfied love need can cause possessiveness and an inability to love appropriately as an adult. Not having this need met brings loneliness, social anxiety, and depression.

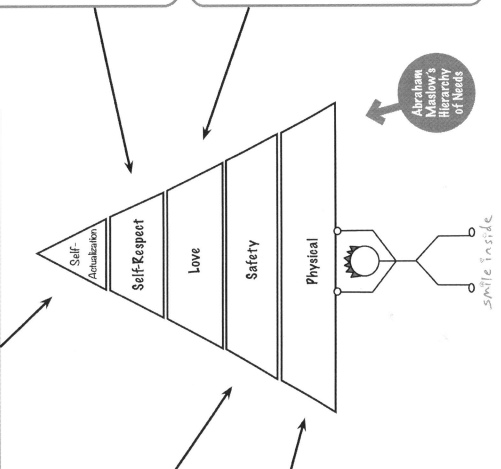

Abraham Maslow's Hierarchy of Needs

Self-Actualization

Self-Respect

Love

Safety

Physical

smile inside

Self-Actualization

Self-actualized people are creative and spontaneous in their ideas and actions. They embrace things in the world with appreciation but can still see things logically and objectively. They have strong values and morals and a gift for solving problems. A person who reaches this state finds happiness and peace in bringing joy to others. Simply put, it is about realizing one's fullest potential.

Those who do not attain this level of self-realization may seem self-centered or apathetic. They have prejudices and lack a strong set of values and morals. They do not strive for personal growth or creative expression.

Unsatisfied or Imbalanced:

Safety

This need is about feeling safe and secure. People want to feel they are safe from harm. This can include a feeling of financial security, having a steady job, or knowing someone is looking after them.

Unsatisfied or Imbalanced:

An unsatisfied safety need brings negative emotions of worry, doubt, and fear.

Physical

These are the most basic of all needs. They include breathing, sleeping, eating, drinking water, urinating, excreting, and having warmth.

Unsatisfied or Imbalanced:

Unsatisfied physical needs leave one dwelling on what the body is lacking. It is difficult to focus on anything else. Not having these needs met can be overwhelming and can cause people to feel sickness, pain, and discomfort.

Needs Analysis

1. These are the ways in which my physical needs have been satisfied:

    _____

    _____

    _____

    _____

    _____

    _____

2. These are the times in which my physical needs have been unsatisfied:

    _____

    _____

    _____

    _____

    _____

3. In the last few months, these people in these ways have helped satisfy my safety need:

    _____

    _____

    _____

    _____

    _____

    _____

4. In the last few months, these people in these ways have hurt my safety need:

5. When I look back over my life, it's obvious that certain people have helped to satisfy my love need. Here are their names and how they have helped:

6. When I look back over my life, it's obvious that certain people have hurt my love need. Here are their names and how they have hurt me:

7. These are my successes and other ways my self-respect need has been satisfied:

8. These are the ways my self-respect need has been hurt:

_____

_____

_____

_____

_____

9. These are my views on being a self-actualized human being:

_____

_____

_____

_____

10. I believe the following people are self-actualized and this is why:

_____

_____

_____

_____

I believe there is a path
From wherever I am to wherever I need to go
That I will be given the light to find that path
That I will be given the strength to follow it
One step at a time
That I will enjoy the journey
And be myself when I arrive

—Author Unknown

smile inside

An Auction of Values

Participants will bid on items at a mock auction, then determine what their choices say about their characters.

materials   *An Auction of Values* handouts, fifteen pretend $100 bills or a substitute (index cards, popsicle sticks, coins) for each participant, journals or paper, pens

> This activity is best done along with *The Power of Choice* (p. 60) and *Auction Analysis* (p. 62) but not necessarily in the same session.

1. Explain to the participants that there will be an auction where they will each have $1,500 of fake money to spend. Pass out the "money" and the *An Auction of Values* handouts.

2. Have them read over all the items silently and then go back and write how much of their $1,500 (in increments of $100) they would be willing to spend on the items that interest them.

3. Explain that the pre-planning exercise was only meant to prepare them for the auction. They can spend their money however they wish once the auction begins.

4. Handle the bidding like an auctioneer, create your own style, or ask a participant to run it. As the auction progresses, be prepared for participants to pool their money in order to buy an item together.

5. When the auction is over and all items have been awarded, have the participants list in their journals what items they desired and what they acquired. Have them respond to the following questions in writing:

    - Why were you willing to spend the majority of your money on _____?
    - Why was it important for you to acquire the other items you bid on?
    - What do your choices in the auction say about your character?

"Let us not look back in anger or forward in fear, but around in awareness."

—James Thurber

An Auction of Values was adapted from an activity in *A Handbook of Personal Growth Activities for the Classroom* by R. and I. Hawley (n.d.).

smile inside

An Auction of Values

1. _____ to be an excellent athlete

2. _____ to be considered a loving person

3. _____ to stop the pollution on our planet

4. _____ to be known as the most fashionable person in the world

5. _____ to be the smartest person in the world

6. _____ to have a lifetime's supply of all my favorite sweets

7. _____ to be able to read minds

8. _____ to never experience any pain or suffering

9. _____ to never have to work

10. _____ to decide the punishments for all criminal offences

11. _____ to make peace in the world

12. _____ to have everyone in my family get along with each other

13. _____ to have a perfect memory

14. _____ to be the richest person in the world

15. _____ to be the leader of the United Nations

16. _____ to interview God

17. _____ to know all the secrets of the universe

18. _____ to be successful at everything I do

19. _____ to be guaranteed a fun party every weekend

20. _____ to travel and learn about all the world's religions

21. _____ to live in a beautiful mansion

22. _____ to spend a month on 'pleasure island' with anyone I choose

23. _____ to enforce laws that give women the same rights as men globally

24. _____ to own the most property in the world

25. _____ to always have someone in my life to love me

26. _____ to be the most popular person everywhere I go all my life

27. _____ to have a huge family

28. _____ to have a perfect body

29. _____ to be able to play video games at any time

30. _____ to always have fun

31. _____ to never look older than 25

32. _____ to be able to heal the people in my family with my hands

33. _____ to free the world of all diseases

34. _____ to be Hollywood's most valuable star

35. _____ to build decent houses for all people

36. _____ to always be happy

37. _____ to see that people of all races are treated fairly and equally

38. _____ to be able to laugh at life

39. _____ to be able to fly

40. _____ to donate as much money as needed to care for the hungry

> ## "Action expresses priorities."
>
> —Mahatma Gandhi

smile inside

The Power of Choice

Participants will rank the importance of a set of life choices. They will write essays describing what they believe they are searching for in life and how they plan to achieve their dreams.

materials   *The Power of Choice* handouts, journals or paper, pens

> This activity is best done after *An Auction of Values* (p. 57) and before *Auction Analysis* (p. 62) but not necessarily in the same session.

1. Pass out the handouts and clarify the meanings of the topics listed if needed.

2. Allow participants time to rank the items according to preference. Have them write their top three on the signs.

3. Have volunteers share their top three with the group.

4. Give the participants the following topic for an essay: *Describe what you believe you are searching for in life and how you plan on achieving your dreams.*

5. Respond in writing to their essays.

> *"People are always blaming their circumstances for what they are. I don't believe in circumstances. The people who get on in this world are the people who get up and look for the circumstances they want, and, if they can't find them, make them."*
>
> —George Bernard Shaw

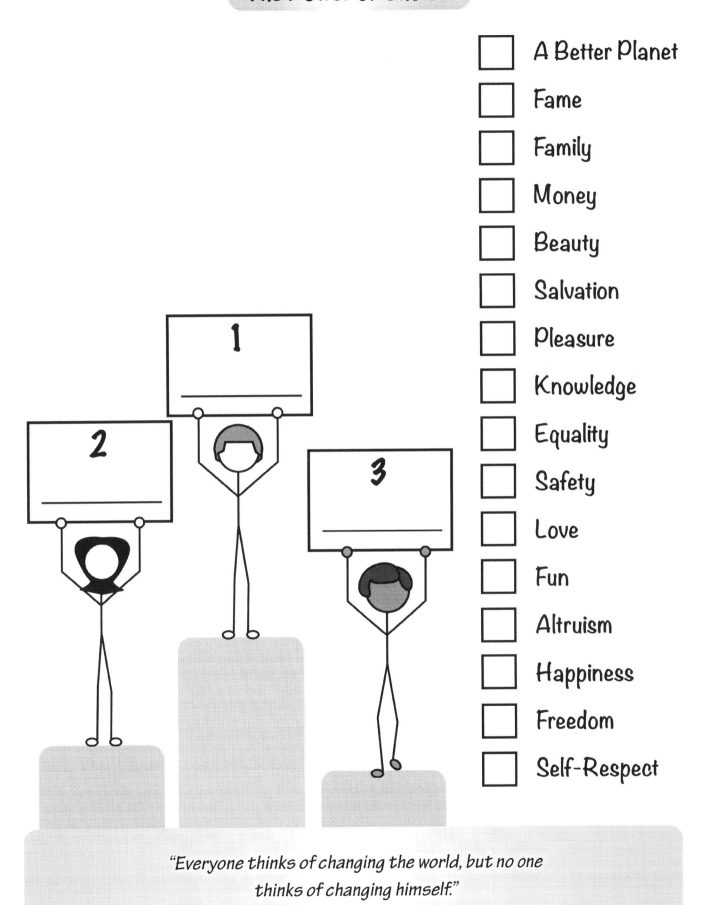

The Power of Choice

- [ ] A Better Planet
- [ ] Fame
- [ ] Family
- [ ] Money
- [ ] Beauty
- [ ] Salvation
- [ ] Pleasure
- [ ] Knowledge
- [ ] Equality
- [ ] Safety
- [ ] Love
- [ ] Fun
- [ ] Altruism
- [ ] Happiness
- [ ] Freedom
- [ ] Self-Respect

"Everyone thinks of changing the world, but no one thinks of changing himself."

—Leo Tolstoy

smile inside

Auction Analysis

Participants will discover if the values they gave priority to during *The Power of Choice* matched their actions during *An Auction of Values*. They will reflect on their choices through discussion and writing.

40 min

materials participant results from *An Auction of Values* and *The Power of Choice* activities, *Values to Virtues* handouts, *Auction Analysis* handouts, journals or paper, pens

This activity must be done after *An Auction of Values* (p. 57) and *The Power of Choice* (p. 60) but not necessarily in the same session.

1. Have participants look at their completed handouts from both *An Auction of Values* and *The Power of Choice*. Now pass out the *Values to Virtues* handouts. Ask them to link the items they bid on during the auction with corresponding life directions from *The Power of Choice* handouts.

2. The templates below can be used to ask the group about their choices:

   * Who won *to make peace in the world, to be the leader of the United Nations,* and *to stop the pollution on our planet* in the auction? Did you have *A Better Planet* as number one on your *Power of Choice* handout?
   * Who had *Salvation* as number one on their *Power of Choice* list? Did you bid on *to interview God, to know all the secrets of the universe,* or *to travel and learn about all the world's religions*?

3. Pass out the *Auction Analysis* handouts. After participants have finished, discuss some of the questions.

Values to Virtues

A Better Planet

- to make peace in the world
- to be the leader of the United Nations
- to stop the pollution on our planet

Fame

- to be known as the most fashionable person in the world
- to be the most popular person everywhere I go all my life
- to be Hollywood's most valuable star

Family

- to have a huge family
- to be able to heal the people in my family with my hands
- to have everyone in my family get along with each other

Money

- to be the richest person in the world
- to live in a beautiful mansion
- to own the most property in the world

Beauty

- to have a perfect body
- to never look older than 25

Salvation

- to interview God
- to know all the secrets of the universe
- to travel and learn about all the world's religions

Pleasure

- to spend a month on 'pleasure island' with anyone I choose
- to have a lifetime's supply of all my favorite sweets

Knowledge

- to be the smartest person in the world
- to be able to read minds
- to have a perfect memory

smile inside

Equality

- to see that people of all races are treated fairly and equally
- to enforce laws that give women the same rights as men globally

Safety

- to never experience any pain or suffering
- to decide the punishments for all criminal offences

Love

- to always have someone in my life to love me
- to be considered a loving person

Fun

- to be guaranteed a fun party every weekend
- to always have fun

Altruism

- to free the world of all diseases
- to build decent houses for all people
- to donate as much money as needed to care for the hungry

Happiness

- to always be happy
- to be able to laugh at life

Freedom

- to never have to work
- to be able to fly
- to be able to play video games at any time

Self-Respect

- to be successful at everything I do
- to be an excellent athlete

Auction Analysis

1. List three items you were willing to spend your entire $1,500 on even if you didn't win them:

   _____

   _____

   _____

2. Why were you willing to spend all of your money on those items?

   _____

   _____

   _____

3. What do those three choices say about your character?

   _____

   _____

   _____

4. List your top three from *The Power of Choice*:

   _____

5. Did the values you bid on during the auction align with your top three choices on *The Power of Choice* handout according to the *Values to Virtues* list? Explain.

   _____

   _____

   _____

6. Do the choices you made in the auction match your priorities in life? How are they the same or different?

   _____

7. If you could participate in the auction again, how would you do things differently?

8. What changes, if any, would you make to your *The Power of Choice* list?

9. Does money equal happiness? Why or why not?

10. Does success equal happiness? Why or why not?

11. How do you believe people should measure their happiness?

12. What is the ultimate goal of life? Did you rank the representation of this value first on your *The Power of Choice* list?

Please Hear That I Am Me

Participants will listen to and analyze two poems with differing perspectives on self. They will discuss the poems and respond to them in writing. They will create artworks that symbolize how they portray themselves to the world and who they truly are.

materials   *Please Hear What I'm Not Saying* poem handouts, *I Am Me poem* handouts, *Reflections* handouts, journals or paper, pens, art supplies

1. Distribute the first poem. Ask for volunteers to each read a stanza of *Please Hear What I'm Not Saying* by Charles C. Finn aloud. Encourage the participants to share what they believe the author is saying.

2. Distribute the second poem. Have a volunteer read *I Am Me* by Virginia Satir aloud. Ask the participants to share what they think the author is saying.

3. Pass out the *Reflections* handouts. Have the participants write their responses to the questions and then hold a group discussion. Alternatively, have them respond to the poems in their journals.

4. Ask the participants to create a piece of artwork titled *The Many Masks of Me*. It should depict the many parts of themselves they show to the world but also who they truly are when they are comfortable and happy.

5. Suggest to participants who are having trouble getting started to sketch some masks and label them with the different roles they play or moods they experience. Encourage them to assign colors to each of those masks as well as to their authentic selves.

6. Give participants time to share and explain their artworks to each other.

Please Hear What I'm Not Saying

Don't be fooled by me.
Don't be fooled by the face I wear
for I wear a mask, a thousand masks,
masks that I'm afraid to take off,
and none of them is me.

Pretending is an art that's second nature with me,
but don't be fooled,
for God's sake don't be fooled.
I give you the impression that I'm secure,
that all is sunny and unruffled with me, within as well
as without,
that confidence is my name and coolness my game,
that the water's calm and I'm in command
and that I need no one,
but don't believe me.
My surface may seem smooth but my surface is my mask,
ever-varying and ever-concealing.
Beneath lies no complacence.
Beneath lies confusion, and fear, and aloneness.
But I hide this. I don't want anybody to know it.
I panic at the thought of my weakness exposed.
That's why I frantically create a mask to hide behind,
a nonchalant sophisticated facade,
to help me pretend,
to shield me from the glance that knows.

But such a glance is precisely my salvation, my only hope,
and I know it.
That is, if it's followed by acceptance,
if it's followed by love.
It's the only thing that can liberate me from myself,
from my own self-built prison walls,
from the barriers I so painstakingly erect.

smile inside

It's the only thing that will assure me
of what I can't assure myself,
that I'm really worth something.
But I don't tell you this. I don't dare to, I'm afraid to.
I'm afraid your glance will not be followed by acceptance,
will not be followed by love.
I'm afraid you'll think less of me,
that you'll laugh, and your laugh would kill me.
I'm afraid that deep down I'm nothing
and that you will see this and reject me.

So I play my game, my desperate pretending game,
with a facade of assurance without
and a trembling child within.
So begins the glittering but empty parade of masks,
and my life becomes a front.

I idly chatter to you in the suave tones of surface talk.
I tell you everything that's really nothing,
and nothing of what's everything,
of what's crying within me.
So when I'm going through my routine
do not be fooled by what I'm saying.
Please listen carefully and try to hear what I'm not saying,
what I'd like to be able to say,
what for survival I need to say,
but what I can't say.

I don't like hiding.
I don't like playing superficial phony games.
I want to stop playing them.
I want to be genuine and spontaneous and me
but you've got to help me.
You've got to hold out your hand
even when that's the last thing I seem to want.
Only you can wipe away from my eyes
the blank stare of the breathing dead.
Only you can call me into aliveness.

smile inside

Each time you're kind, and gentle, and encouraging,
each time you try to understand because you really care,
my heart begins to grow wings—
very small wings,
very feeble wings,
but wings!

With your power to touch me into feeling
you can breathe life into me.
I want you to know that.
I want you to know how important you are to me,
how you can be a creator—an honest-to-God creator—
of the person that is me
if you choose to.
You alone can break down the wall behind which I tremble,
you alone can remove my mask,
you alone can release me from my shadow-world of panic,
from my lonely prison,
if you choose to.
Please choose to.

Do not pass me by.
It will not be easy for you.
A long conviction of worthlessness builds strong walls.
The nearer you approach to me
the blinder I may strike back.
It's irrational, but despite what the books say about man
often I am irrational.
I fight against the very thing I cry out for.
But I am told that love is stronger than strong walls
and in this lies my hope.
Please try to beat down those walls
with firm hands but with gentle hands
for a child is very sensitive.

Who am I, you may wonder?
I am someone you know very well.
For I am every man you meet
and I am every woman you meet.

—Charles C. Finn, 1966

(Used with permission from Charles C. Finn, www.poetrybycharlescfinn.com.)

smile inside

I AM ME

IN ALL THE WORLD, THERE IS NO ONE ELSE EXACTLY LIKE ME
EVERYTHING THAT COMES OUT OF ME IS AUTHENTICALLY MINE
BECAUSE I ALONE CHOSE IT—I OWN EVERYTHING ABOUT ME
MY BODY, MY FEELINGS, MY MOUTH, MY VOICE, ALL MY ACTIONS,
WHETHER THEY BE TO OTHERS OR TO MYSELF—I OWN MY FANTASIES,
MY DREAMS, MY HOPES, MY FEARS—I OWN ALL MY TRIUMPHS AND
SUCCESSES, ALL MY FAILURES AND MISTAKES—BECAUSE I OWN ALL OF ME,
I CAN BECOME INTIMATELY ACQUAINTED WITH ME—BY SO DOING I CAN LOVE ME
AND BE FRIENDLY WITH ME IN ALL MY PARTS—I KNOW THERE ARE ASPECTS OF
MYSELF THAT PUZZLE ME, AND OTHER ASPECTS THAT I DO NOT KNOW—BUT AS
LONG AS I AM FRIENDLY AND LOVING TO MYSELF, I CAN COURAGEOUSLY AND
HOPEFULLY LOOK FOR SOLUTIONS TO THE PUZZLES AND FOR WAYS TO FIND
OUT MORE ABOUT ME—HOWEVER I LOOK AND SOUND, WHATEVER I SAY AND DO
AND WHATEVER I THINK AND FEEL AT A GIVEN MOMENT IN TIME IS AUTHENTICALLY
ME—IF LATER SOME PARTS OF HOW I LOOKED, SOUNDED, THOUGHT AND FELT
TURN OUT TO BE UNFITTING, I CAN DISCARD THAT WHICH IS UNFITTING, KEEP
THE REST, AND INVENT SOMETHING NEW FOR THAT WHICH I DISCARDED—I
CAN SEE, HEAR, FEEL, THINK, SAY, AND DO. I HAVE THE TOOLS TO SURVIVE,
TO BE CLOSE TO OTHERS, TO BE PRODUCTIVE, AND TO MAKE SENSE AND
ORDER OUT OF THE WORLD OF PEOPLE AND THINGS OUTSIDE OF ME
—I OWN ME, AND THEREFORE I CAN ENGINEER ME—
I AM ME AND I AM OKAY

Virginia Satir, 1975

smile inside

Reflections

What do you think Charles C. Finn is trying to say?

_____

_____

What do you think Virginia Satir is trying to say?

_____

_____

How are the poems the same? Different?

_____

_____

_____

Do you think who you are is a tangible thing, an intangible thing, or both? Explain.

_____

_____

If the author of the first poem never took off his masks, how do you predict his life would turn out?

_____

_____

What are some signs that someone may need us to reach out to them?

_____

_____

Is it easy for you to express love to the people you care about most? How do you show them?

_____

_____

_____

When is it most difficult for you to be yourself? Why?

_____

_____

Do you love yourself? Why or why not?

Why do you think it's important to have the freedom to reinvent yourself as often as you like?

If someone is happy with who they are and is not interested in self-improvement, should that wish be respected? What if that person is causing others distress or suffering?

Does everyone deserve to be loved? Why or why not?

Should people be encouraged to improve themselves? Why or why not? How can this happen without offending anyone?

Do you think you will make it a point to improve who you are as a person continually?
Why or why not?

ME Day

Participants will give presentations on themselves to their peers.
They will draw further information from those presenting.

materials   facilitator presentation items, *ME Day* handouts, list of future dates for the presentations, audio-visual equipment to present slide shows or music, napkins

1. Introduce this activity by giving a ten-minute presentation on yourself. Then play your favorite music and present a slide show or pass around photographs.

2. Share your favorite snack and open the floor for a question-and-answer session. Encourage participants to ask thoughtful questions about things that interested them during the presentation.

3. Distribute the handouts and have all participants sign up for days to give their presentations.

4. If your group doesn't have a lot of time together, a condensed version of this activity without photos, music, and a snack will also work well. If you have a lot of time together, participants could creatively plan for twenty-minute presentations. Encourage them to tell stories, show a home video, speak in depth about one of their interests or teach the group something they know a lot about through a short demonstration (e.g., performing arts, martial arts, craft).

"It is better to be hated for what you are than loved for what you are not. But it is best to be loved for what you are."

—Author Unknown

ME Day

You are responsible for a multi-media presentation about yourself.

BRING:

- Photographs (from your childhood, of family, of friends, from school, of holidays, etc.) or a slide show.
- Your favorite music.
- Awards or trophies you won.
- Your creations (e.g., drawings, paintings, models, clothes sculptures, collages, cross-stitch, poems, stories).
- Your favorite snack food—to share.

Present yourself answering all of these questions:

1. When and where were you born?
2. Have you lived in the same place your whole life?
3. If you've moved, where have you lived?
4. What is your earliest memory?
5. What schools have you attended?
6. What did you like and dislike about your previous schools?
7. What did you think about high school at first?
8. How have you changed since then?
9. What are your interests now?
10. What are your goals in life?

"Have confidence that if you have done a little thing well, you can do a bigger thing well too."

—David Storey

smile inside

EMOTIONS & COPING

How important it is to be heard! Not just heard but listened to and truly understood. Equally important is knowing how to speak from the heart. The teenage years are full of highs and lows with surges of emotions that affect relationships and one's sense of self. Being given the option for self-expression can be a cathartic experience. *Complete the Thought* (p. 78) and *Boundary Breaking* (p. 80) allow participants to engage in meaningful conversations wherein they can share feelings, thoughts, and memories.

Melodic Moods (p. 82) and *Health Is Wealth* (p. 83) help participants gain insight into how external factors, emotions, and stress affect the body, state of mind, and behavior. This knowledge goes a long way in helping one maintain sound physical and mental health.

Having the tools necessary to cope with challenges is also crucial. Participants get the chance to explore and practice various coping techniques during *Stressed Out? Try This!* (p. 89). With tool-kits packed full of healthy coping strategies, young people will be less likely to form self-destructive habits in the future.

Complete the Thought

Participants will complete statements and share their personal feelings and thoughts with partners. They will respectfully listen to their partners.

materials *Complete the Thought* handouts, pens

1. Pass out the *Complete the Thought* handouts. Ask the participants to write the first thing that comes to mind in response to the prompts.

2. Assure participants they will not have to share the responses they would like to keep private. Allow them ample time to finish.

3. Ask all participants to find a partner. Remind everyone to listen with compassion and to respect each other's differences as they share their responses.

4. Affirm that accepting diversity means that every person should be celebrated for the unique individual he or she is.

> *"We don't always know what makes us happy.*
> *We know, instead, what we think SHOULD.*
> *We are baffled and confused when our attempts at happiness fail...*
> *We are mute when it comes to naming accurately*
> *our own preferences, delights, gifts, talents.*
> *The voice of our original self is often muffled, overwhelmed,*
> *even strangled, by the voices of other people's expectations.*
> *The tongue of the original self is the language of the heart."*

—Julia Cameron

Complete the Thought

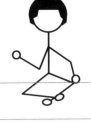

1. I am a person who _____

2. One of the things I would like people to know about me is _____

3. When I try to talk about things that are important to me _____

4. I am beginning to suspect _____

5. One of the things I had to do to survive _____

6. I am becoming aware of _____

7. All my life I have felt _____

8. It is not easy for me to admit that _____

9. If I did not have to worry about my image _____

10. If I allowed myself to just enjoy who I am _____

11. If I were honest right now I would _____

12. One of the ways I might sabotage my positive feelings is _____

13. One of the things I would like to be valued and appreciated for is _____

14. I hurt myself by _____

15. In the future, I _____

16. One of the things I would like to know about me is _____

17. If you really knew me, you would _____

18. Right now, I am afraid that _____

19. I will not _____

20. I pretend that _____

21. One of the things I wish people understood about me is _____

22. I tell myself _____

> *"There's nothing so rewarding as to make people realize they are worthwhile in this world."*
>
> – Bob Anderson

smile inside

Boundary Breaking

Participants will answer personal questions and listen to their peers' responses. They will discuss their experiences and make observations.

1. Read or paraphrase the following instructions:

> This activity is *Boundary Breaking,* a group interaction experience. I will ask you to respond to a series of questions. Every answer is right. No one will challenge any answers. Just respond to what you hear. Make every answer your own. Try not to give the same answer as someone else and try not to change your answer after you've thought of it. You don't need to try to find appropriate answers. Just be honestly aware of your own thoughts and feelings.
>
> We will proceed around the circle, starting with a different person each time. If you don't have an answer at your turn, you can pass. We'll come back to you later. Speak so everyone can hear you. When you're not answering, look at the person who is speaking. We can learn things from others' expressions and movements as well as their words.
>
> Our concern now is to discover good things about each other. We are here to listen, not to debate or disagree. We're here to find our own strengths and to recognize the strengths of the people around us.
>
> As the other people speak, collect their answers in your mind. Begin to really understand and know each person here. If we all do this, perhaps a few of our invisible boundaries will begin to break and we will begin to know each other as real people.

2. Ask the Boundary Breaking Questions on the opposite page preferably in the order listed. The questions that require deeper thought are listed after the icebreaking questions. Allow the participants to explain their answers if they choose to, but keep it optional. Depending on the size and dynamics of the group, the activity may be more successful if the participants are in small groups.

3. Conclude *Boundary Breaking* by using the Synthesis Questions for reflection.

"The most important things are the hardest to say. They are the things you get ashamed of, because words diminish them—words shrink things that seem limitless when they were in your head to no more than living size when they're brought out. ...That's the worst I think. When the secret stays locked within not for want of a teller but for want of an understanding ear."

—Stephen King

smile inside

Boundary Breaking Questions

- What is the best movie you've ever seen and why?
- If you could be an animal, what would you be?
- If you could travel anywhere in the world, where would you go first?
- What person has influenced your life the most?
- What do you like to do most with free time?
- What's the most beautiful thing you've ever seen?
- When do you feel most lonely?
- When do you feel most alive?
- What future discovery do you hope for most?
- What will you be doing twenty years from today?
- What is your strongest emotion?
- What would you like to change about yourself?
- What do you like best about yourself?
- What do you like best about your family?
- What are you proud of that you have accomplished?
- What's the best gift you've ever received?
- What are you doing to improve yourself?
- If your house was on fire, what would you save first?
- My most important rule for living is...
- When people first see me, they...
- The way I'm generous with others is...
- An important value for me is...
- I like people who...
- People who really know me think...
- What I distrust most is...
- The most important thing I learned this year is...
- Something that holds me back is...
- I laugh when...
- I cry when...
- I wish...

Synthesis Questions

- Which person did you learn the most about?
- Which person do you want to know more about?
- Which person surprised you the most?
- What did you notice about body language?
- What did you observe about listening skills?
- Did you wonder why people answered the way they did sometimes?
- Do you think you'll ask those people about their answers later?
- What do you think about this boundary breaking experience?

smile inside

Melodic Moods

Participants will reflect on their emotional responses to selections of music. They will compare their emotional and logical interpretations of the music. They will discuss the impact music has on emotions and society.

materials   Six songs/pieces of instrumental music from diverse genres, music player, journals or paper, pens

1. Explain to the participants that they are about to hear a selection of music. They are to reflect on each individual piece and think about how it makes them feel. In addition, they are to decide what message they think the artist(s) means to convey.

2. Ask everyone to write their thoughts in their journals as they listen to each piece of music. Play the music and give the participants one minute of reflection time between songs.

3. Ask some participants to share what they wrote about the last piece of music played.

4. Ask the group:

   - Which pieces portray feelings of celebration and joy?
   - Which pieces portray feelings of frustration or anger?
   - Which pieces excite you? Relax you?
   - Which pieces evoke empathy? Hate?
   - Which pieces have lyrics that are arrogant? Humble?

5. Replay samples of the songs and discuss. Ask the participants to decide if their emotional response is comparable to their interpretation of the song's message.

6. Ask the group:

   - How much is music a part of your life?
   - How does music affect your mood?
   - How much of an impact does music have on society? Give examples.

"Feelings are much like waves, we can't stop them from coming but we can choose which one to surf."

- Jonatan Mårtensson

Health is Wealth

Participants will identify the effects stress has on the body, emotions, and mind and give examples of stressors. They will explain how a variety of healthy coping strategies affect different levels of being and debate how they could be categorized.
They will chose new coping strategies to try in the future.

materials a visual aid, *Coping Cards*, tape, journals or paper, pens

1. Brainstorm a list of feelings that are warning signs of stress. This can be done with the entire group or have the participants break up into small groups or partners. Possible answers:

   - Irritable
   - Worried
   - Anxious
   - Afraid
   - Frustrated
   - Overwhelmed
   - Nervous
   - Sad
   - Confused
   - Angry
   - Helpless
   - Inadequate

2. Have participants brainstorm reasons why they may feel stressed. Possible answers:

   - Peer pressure
   - Parents expecting perfect grades
   - Disagreements with friends
   - Siblings are irritating
   - Being teased or bullied
   - Having too much to do
   - Making important decisions
   - Facing difficulty or crisis
   - Relationship issues
   - Problems at home
   - Moving to a new house
   - Having fears

3. Explain that stress can build up in the body and cause physical, emotional, and mental symptoms when it's not addressed. Write the word *disease* on the visual aid. Draw a line between the s and the e (dis/ease). Ask the group to explain what that means (dis=not, ease=being relaxed, therefore disease=not being relaxed). In order to decrease the likelihood of disease, one must learn to reduce the stress in their life.

4. Make three columns with the headings Physical, Emotional, and Mental. Ask participants to give examples of how not coping with stress can affect the body, heart, and mind in the short and long terms.

   Possible answers for Physical:

   - Racing heart
   - Sweating
   - Shaky
   - Ulcers
   - Nausea
   - Stomach pain
   - Weight loss/gain
   - Headaches
   - Smoking
   - Drug/alcohol addiction
   - High blood pressure
   - Nervousness
   - Muscle pain
   - Illness
   - Insomnia
   - Oversleeping
   - Loss of appetite
   - Rashes

Possible answers for Emotional:

- Panic attacks
- Anger
- Depression
- Mood swings

- Anxiety
- Crying
- Violence
- Tantrums

Possible answers for Mental:

- Lack of confidence
- Negative thoughts
- Apathy
- Forgetfulness

- Lying
- Isolating oneself
- Clouded thinking
- Saying things you don't really mean

5. Explain that in order to stay physically, emotionally, and mentally healthy, one must not let stress take over. Equate getting stressed out with "falling apart." In order to put the pieces back together, one needs to have the tools to do this. Healthy coping strategies are the tools used to repair the damage to the different levels of being, but they can also prevent one from falling apart in the first place.

6. Create a large two by two grid on a visual aid with the headings Physical, Emotional, Mental, and Spiritual. State that coping strategies can support more than one level of being, but they tend to benefit one level more than the others.

7. Give one Coping Card to each participant. Have participants, one at a time, affix their cards in the category they believe the coping strategy will benefit the most and to justify their decisions.

8. Allow the rest of the participants to either agree or debate after each placement. Participants may change their minds or want to place their cards on the lines between categories after the discussion.

9. Once everyone has had a turn and if there is time, categorize the remaining Coping Cards with the group.

10. Ask participants to write in their journals why the coping techniques they normally use suit them and to list four new strategies, one from each level, they plan to try in the future.

11. This activity is about generating discussion and debate so the participants can become more familiar with a variety of coping strategies. The cards on the following pages have been categorized according to how they may most benefit each level of being, but this is to be used as an approximate framework to assist in facilitating the discussion. There are no right answers as each person is unique in how a strategy may benefit them the most.

"Every human being is the author of his own health or disease."

—Sivananda

Exercise

Eat Healthy

Get a massage

Breathe deeply

Stretch to release tension

Get some fresh air

Take time out to relax or have a nap

Avoid stressful situations

Have a bath

Go to bed early

Spend time with a pet	*Do something fun with someone you love*
Talk to someone	**Cry**
Listen to music that makes you feel **GOOD**	*Be creative* (art, music, poetry, etc.)
Watch a comedy	Punch a pillow
Eliminate negativity from your life	*Write in a journal*

Start saying "no" to simplify your social life

Quiet your mind and be open to a solution that may help you

Change your thinking

Reduce your stress through lifestyle changes

Consistently set aside time in your schedule to be alone

MAKE A PLAN TO IMPROVE THE WAY YOU DEAL WITH STRESS

Prioritize your to-do list

Manage your time better

Practice optimism

Replace unhealthy coping strategies with healthy ones

PRAY

GO TO CHURCH/TEMPLE

Meditate

HAVE FAITH

Think to yourself, "everything happens for a reason"

Talk to someone you trust about spirituality

Participate in service work that helps those in need

Sing songs of worship

Read religious or spiritual texts

Trust that life is happening just the way it should

Stressed Out? Try This!

Participants will practice different coping techniques to reduce stress.

materials   unscented hand lotion, relaxing music, music player

Explore a few different stress-reduction techniques with the group, such as:

Massage Techniques

Form a standing circle. Ask each person to put his or her hands on the shoulders of the person to his or her right and give that person a massage. After a minute or two, change directions. Now ask everyone to find a scalp-and-hand massage partner. Instruct one member of each pair to lie on the floor on their back while their partner sits cross-legged at their head. Tell the individual sitting to lift their partner's head carefully, supporting its weight. Have them proceed to make small circles with their fingers all over the scalp, avoiding the temple area on either side of the head. Then they should make stroking motions with their fingers from the base of the neck to the hairline while supporting the head with the base of their palms. After a few minutes, have the masseur carefully lower their partner's head and end the session by gently massaging the ear lobes. Ask the partners to switch positions and repeat the instructions.

Next, distribute the lotion and have the partners give each other hand massages. The hands are the most used part of the body but the least nurtured. Recommend they use their thumbs to push the skin from the base of the palm toward the fingers. Then have everyone massage their partners' fingers from the knuckles to the tips using a firm, pulling motion.

Laughter Release

Conduct a spontaneous laughter circle. Explain that laughter is an excellent outlet for stress. Start by asking everyone to think of something they find really funny and laugh out loud. Encourage them to try new ways of laughing or to make sounds like "Ha! Ha! Ha!" using their abdominal muscles.

Stretching

Tell the group they're going to take a stress test. Ask everyone to raise one arm high above their head, then ask them to notice if their opposite shoulder is tensed or relaxed. Explain that being aware of unnecessary tension will help them function in a more relaxed manner. Give the group some time to stretch their muscles in ways they have previously learned in sports, physical education, or dance classes. Ask everyone to try the exercise again with their other arm, this time being aware of the tension in their opposite shoulder. Challenge everyone to be aware of how they tense their muscles unnecessarily when they engage in simple activities like using a computer or talking on the phone. Encourage them to be as relaxed as possible while they carry out activities in their daily lives.

Deep Relaxation

Each participant needs to have their own space on the floor to lie down on their back with their legs slightly apart and arms slightly away from the body. Start playing music while they're getting settled. Then read the Deep Relaxation script (p.116) aloud in a soft and slow voice.

smile inside

PROBLEM SOLVING & DECISION MAKING

An effective problem solver is open-minded in their approach, flexible in their method, and creative in their solution. If young people are given the opportunity to practice inductive and deductive thinking, their ability to solve problems successfully will improve.

Use the brain-stretching riddles in this module to get participants thinking laterally, upside down, and outside of the box. Further expand their capabilities with *Head vs. Heart* (p. 97), in which participants explore the effectiveness of various problem-solving methods when confronted with logical and emotional issues.

It's estimated that an individual makes hundreds of decisions every day. Most of these are done unconsciously, but what about the big ones? The realizations and skills that participants have gained up to this point will form a strong basis for good decision making, but in order to make even wiser decisions young people should practice skills such as having foresight, verbalizing why a decision has been made, and having the humility to seek new information—all of which are addressed in the remaining activities.

In *Where Do You Stand?* (p. 99), participants are asked to provide their reasoning behind opinions they make public. *Think, Predict, Act* (p. 100) has them weighing pros and cons and predicting consequences. In *Deserted Island* (p. 102) participants learn to revise decisions after seeking the opinions of their peers. Finally, *What to Do?* (p. 103) tests the participant's conviction to remain true to their values through moral dilemmas.

Participants will figure out a hidden physical pattern.

materials   two spoons, sticks or pens

1. This activity works best if everyone is seated in a circle of chairs. Explain that you are all going to play a game that involves solving a riddle. Request that as each person figures out the secret, they do not ruin it for others by sharing. Emphasize the importance of allowing others to challenge their minds so they can earn the rewards of personal achievement.

2. Pass two spoons around the circle. Request that each person hold them in a random position and then answer the question which is a riddle.

3. Ask each person, "Is the answer crossed or uncrossed?" and then approve or disapprove of his or her answer.

4. The secret is that the answer of being "crossed" or "uncrossed" has to do with the position of the participant's legs, not the spoons. If their legs are crossed when it's their turn, the answer is "crossed." If their legs are uncrossed, the answer is "uncrossed."

5. Continue to ask the question over one or more sessions until everyone figures it out.

> "This is an unusual paragraph. I am curious how quickly you can find out what is so unusual about it. It looks so plain you would think nothing was wrong with it. In actual fact, nothing is wrong with it! It is unusual, though. Study it and think about it, but you still may not find anything odd. But if you work at it a bit, you might find out. Don't look at the small print until you think long and hard!"

(The unusual thing is the letter e is nowhere to be found!)

1. Tell the group one or more of the following riddles:

   - There is a person lying down in the desert, stomach to the ground, with a backpack on. The person is dead. What happened? (His parachute didn't open.)

   - What runs away as fast as you run to it until it eventually dies of thirst? (A rainbow.)

   - The person who made it doesn't need it. The person who bought it won't use it. The person who used it didn't know it. What is it? (A coffin.)

   - There's a man who lives on the top floor of a very tall building. Every day he takes the elevator to the ground floor to go to work. Upon returning from work, he can only travel halfway up in the elevator and has to walk the rest of the way unless it's raining! Why? (He's too short to reach the button in the elevator for his floor unless he has his umbrella with him.)

   - A man walks into a bar and asks the bartender for a glass of water. The bartender pulls out a gun and points it at the man. The man says "thank you" and walks out. Why? (The man had hiccups.)

   - A man turns out the light, walks downstairs, goes home, turns on the television, gets a gun out, and shoots himself. What happened and why did he do it? (He worked in a lighthouse and accidentally switched off the light. When he got home he saw on the news that a ship had crashed on his shore and many lives were lost. He felt so guilty for his mistake, he did not want to live anymore.)

   - What's black when you buy it, red when you use it, and gray when you throw it away? (Charcoal.)

2. The participants may ask only yes-no questions to gather clues to the mysteries. They may discuss possible answers amongst themselves to deduce solutions by reasoning.

3. Encourage participants to whisper the answers in your ear when they think they have figured out the riddle so everyone has a chance to be sleuths at their own pace.

4. Find more riddles by searching for "lateral thinking puzzles" on the Internet.

The Big Picture

Participants will discover the hidden pattern behind a game.

materials   ten pens or markers

1. Explain that you are all going to play a game that involves solving a riddle. Request that as each person figures out the secret, they do not ruin it for others by sharing. Emphasize the importance of allowing others to challenge their minds so they can earn the rewards of personal achievement.

2. Sitting on the floor or standing at a table, toss ten pens down where everyone can see.

3. After tossing the pens, discreetly touch a chosen number of your fingertips to the floor or table. Ask the group to look at the big picture and determine what number they see. The group will study the pens, trying to figure out the pattern. The number of fingers touching the floor or table is the answer.

4. Begin to give clues if no one catches on:

   - Remember the name of the game is *The Big Picture*.
   - Look all around. The answer doesn't always lie right in front of you.
   - Be exaggerated in the way you display your fingers.

5. Test the individuals who believe they've discovered the secret by requiring three correct guesses in a row.

6. This is a good game to play when there are five minutes to spare. Persist until everyone figures it out.

"Nothing is impossible; we merely do not know yet how to do it."

—Author Unknown

The Little Picture

Participants will discover the hidden pattern behind a game.

materials   nine blank pieces of paper, a pen

1. Explain that you are all going to play a game that involves solving a riddle. Request that as each person figures out the secret, they do not ruin it for others by sharing. Emphasize the importance of allowing others to challenge their minds so they can earn the rewards of personal achievement.

2. Lay the pieces of paper out in a three by three grid. Make sure all the participants can see all nine pieces of paper.

3. Say you're thinking of a particular piece of paper in the grid and that participants will be able to guess the correct one if they pay attention to the little picture.

4. With the chosen piece in mind, touch the pen to one piece of paper at a time, precisely in the spot that will reveal the secret. If you secretly chose the middle piece of paper, point to the middle of each piece of paper you touch and ask, "Is it this one?" each time. Have them guess "yes" or "no" until you touch the correct one and can say "correct" or "it is this one." If you are thinking of the piece of paper in the upper right corner of the grid, touch the upper right corner of each piece of paper while asking again and again, "Is it this one?" Continue the process until everyone catches on.

5. Begin to give clues if no one catches on:

    o Remember the name of the game is *The Little Picture.*
    o Watch the pen closely.
    o Notice the grid within the grid.
    o Begin marking the paper with a dot each time the pen touches.

6. Test individuals who believe they have discovered the secret by requiring three correct guesses in a row.

7. This is a good game to play when there are five minutes to spare.

Snapps

Participants will decipher the secret code behind a game.

1. There must be two people who know the secret to play the game. A preparation session with one of the group members and yourself is required for the activity to be successful.

2. Explain the Secret Code Alphabet below and the following rules only to your partner:

   • I will ask a participant to whisper the name of a well-known person to me.
   • I will relay the answer to you through a secret language. It will appear as if I am snapping a code to you with my fingers, but the answer lies in the first letter of every phrase I say between snaps.
   • Here is an example for the name Rachel. (Speak directly to your partner. Act like you are concentrating on your actions which helps draw attention to the snapping.)

   > **R**eady? (Snap your fingers one or more times.)
   > **A**lright. (Snap your fingers one or more times.)
   > **C**ome on! (Snap your fingers one or more times.)
   > **H**ere we go. (Snap your fingers one or more times.)
   > **E**ach snap is separate. (Snap your fingers one or more times.)
   > **L**et's not get confused. (Snap your fingers one or more times.)

   • I will always spell the last name first to make it easier for you. I will say "remember the name of the game is *Snapps*" to indicate when I am starting a new word. When you know the name, say it aloud.

3. After the training session, in front of the group with your partner, ask a participant to whisper the name of a well-known person in your ear. Conduct *Snapps* according to the Secret Code Alphabet suggestions or make up your own. Challenge the group to discover the secret of the game.

4. When someone understands the secret, have them whisper it to you so everyone else has a fair chance to solve the riddle.

Secret Code Alphabet

A.....Alright!	**N**......Not again!
B...... Be careful.	**O**......Oh!
C.....Come on!	**P**.......Please…
D.....Don't mess this up.	**Q**......Quickly, please!
E......Each snap is separate.	**R**.......Ready?
F......Figure this out!	**S**.......So close!
G.....Get this please!	**T**.......Try again.
H.....Here we go (again)!	**U**......Understand?
I.....I think you have it!	**V**......Very close.
J......Just don't give up!	**W**.....What?
K.....Keep it up.	**X**......X-cellent!
L......Let's not get confused.	**Y**.......You are good!
M.....Maybe…	**Z**.....Zilch!

Substitute whatever words come naturally. As long as the first letter of the phrase matches the intended clue, the game will be successful.

Head vs. Heart

Participants will examine the effectiveness of problem-solving methods for logical and emotional problems.

materials   access to the Internet, journals or paper, pens

1. Divide the participants into small groups.

2. Give the following assignment:

> Every group must research a unique problem-solving method on the Internet. Come up with an actual, logic-based problem and one emotion-based to solve or choose hypothetical problems. Demonstrate to the rest of the group in a presentation how both of these problems could be solved using the method you've chosen.

Logic-based problems

- The litter problem at the local park is most likely caused by teenagers who think they own it on the weekends.
- Students are exiting primary school without being able to read properly.
- There's traffic congestion when students are being dropped off at school in the morning.
- More people are dying from health issues related to obesity than ever before.
- You volunteer at the local pet shelter, which is now at capacity.

Emotion-based problems

- Your sister is being cyber-bullied and doesn't want to tell anyone.
- Your parents are divorcing and have asked you to decide if you're going to live with your mother or father.
- Your best friend is addicted to video games and doesn't talk to you anymore because of it.
- You are experiencing depression over the death of a pet.
- Both of your friends like the same person (who is also your friend) and are fighting over him or her. You're stuck in the middle of the whole thing.

3. Share an example using the POOCH problem-solving method:

> **P**roblem (Define it.)
> **O**ptions (What are the possible solutions?)
> **O**utcome (What are the probable outcomes for each option?)
> **C**hoose (Which is the best option?)
> **H**ow did it go? (Reflect.)

P: The buses are dropping you and the majority of your classmates off at school late every day.

O: Ask the bus driver to start his rounds earlier, get the bus company to send more buses, or get the school administrators to start the day later.

O: The bus company might not be able to do the first two options, but we can ask, and the same goes for the school.

C: Find out who has the most flexibility and is willing to help and choose that option.

H: The bus company would not budge for many reasons, but the school administrators said they would move homeroom from the end of the day to the start so no one would miss any class time. We discovered there was a reasonable solution that hadn't even crossed our minds. It's good to explore options and stay flexible.

Emotion-based problem example

P: Someone in our group works at the snack bar at the local pool. The older kids are cutting in front of the younger kids all the time. The younger kids get upset and come crying to her. This makes her upset, especially since her little sister is among them.

O: Ask the older kids to stop, refuse to serve anyone who cuts in line, or create two different lines (one for twelve and under, one for thirteen and older).

O: If she asks the older kids to stop, they may just continue which could get ugly, and they would have to be constantly monitored. Refusing to serve line jumpers means angry customers, creating enemies, and a loss of profit for the snack bar: plus it's hard to monitor. We could easily create a system of two lines with colored rope and two signs. It may or may not work; we'll have to try it out.

C: Try creating two lines.

H: We tried it on the weekend and it was successful. There are still kids (younger and older) who give their money to friends who are already in line, but it isn't such a problem anymore. The younger kids aren't getting upset and neither are the snack bar employees.

4. Set a time limit and have each group showcase their processes for solving both problems in a presentation. Ask each group to decide if its method is more effective solving logic-based or emotion-based problems.

5. Ask the group:

   - Were any of the problems based in both logic and emotion? Explain.
   - Which method do you think works best overall for problems based in both logic and emotion? Why?

6. If the participants chose to solve real problems, schedule the presentations for the following session so they have time to explore the options.

Where Do You Stand?

Participants will form opinions about where they stand on different issues and justify their decisions.

1. Create an Agree/Disagree spectrum within the room by making one wall Strongly Agree and the opposite wall Strongly Disagree. Designate the middle of the room as neutral.

2. Explain to the group that when a statement is read aloud, they must decide where they stand on the spectrum in relation to the topic. The more strongly they feel, the closer they should stand to the appropriate wall. If they are undecided, they should stand in the middle of the room.

3. Emphasize the importance of being able to justify their decisions.

4. Read an Agree/Disagree statement aloud:

   - Energy drinks and candy should be available to buy during lunchtime.
   - Primary-school principals should be allowed to spank naughty children.
   - Children should be taken from their parents who physically abuse them.
   - People should go to jail for driving under the influence of alcohol.
   - The drinking age should be lowered.
   - Zoos are unfair to animals.
   - Animals should be tested in laboratories to find cures for human diseases.
   - Abortion should be illegal.
   - It's okay to hunt animals for sport.
   - Refugees should be allowed to integrate into our country unimpeded.
   - Professional athletes who fail drug tests should be banned from playing.
   - Females athletes should be allowed to play professionally on men's teams.

5. After participants decide their positions, ask why they feel the way they do. Be sure to obtain opinions from both ends of the spectrum.

6. Encourage participants to change their positions after hearing their peers' opinions.

7. Ask if anyone can come up with a current issue in which a political leader has had to make a decision to benefit the majority. Have the participants express where they stand on the spectrum in regard to this issue. Open the floor for debate.

8. Invite everyone to contribute statements that concern them.

Think, Predict, Act

Participants will decide on the best course of action for a hypothetical character after examining the character's choices and possible consequences. Participants will reflect upon decisions they have made that brought about undesirable consequences in their lives.

40 min

materials   *Think, Predict, Act* handouts, journals or paper, pens

1. Discuss the interconnectedness of the following terms:

Choices	Options from which to select.
Consequence	An effect or result; something that happens because of an action.
Decision	A resolution after consideration; the result of making up one's mind.

2. Tell the group about the Think, Predict, Act method. When making a decision it's best to think (about choices), predict (possible consequences), then Act (on one's decision).

3. Pass out the *Think, Predict, Act* handouts. Ask the participants to read the story silently. Then break them up into small groups to discuss possible choices and consequences.

4. Each group should share what they believe is the best course of action for the character and why.

5. Ask everyone to think of a decision they have regretted because of the consequences it brought about. Have them write about it in their journals and review their decision with the Think, Predict, Act method. Ask them to list the choices they had and to predict the consequences for each choice. Have them respond in writing to the following:

   • How would your life have been different if you chose choice A? Choice B? Choice C?
   • In hindsight, would you still have made the same decision? Why or why not?
   • If you could have made a different decision, what do you wish you would have done? Why?

6. This may be a very personal reflection exercise for some participants. Advise them that even though they may regret some decisions, it doesn't mean they were necessarily the wrong decisions; sometimes consequences teach a valuable lesson.

7. Respond to their journal writing with sensitivity and commend those who thought deeply about their past.

Think, Predict, Act

Meaghan just moved to a new school and was having problems making new friends. Everyone seemed to be in tight groups with no interest in having any newcomers join their circles. She didn't know what it took to be part of a group at this school. She had been on the debate team at her previous school and won many awards, but her classmates got jealous and made her life miserable. When the teacher who organized the debate team at her new school heard how good Meaghan was, he asked her to join. Meaghan immediately declined because she didn't want the same thing to happen again. She had promised herself she would do things differently this time and besides, she was having enough problems already.

Meaghan tried her best to fit in but had no luck. One Friday, while eating lunch alone, a cute guy from her psychology class approached her. He introduced himself as Daniel and said, "Follow me. I want to show you something." Meaghan obliged with butterflies in her stomach, in shock that someone was actually talking to her— and that it was Daniel. She'd had her eye on him since her first day at the school.
He made small talk as they made their way across the football field and across another field leading to the woods. Meaghan asked where they were going. Lunch was almost over and they definitely were not on school property anymore. She started to get nervous, and Daniel sensed this. He reassured her that they were almost there.

As they made their way through the trees, she heard the sound of flowing water growing stronger and stronger. Daniel led her over a ridge and down to a river. She was in awe of the peace it instilled in her. She smiled and said, "Thank you for bringing me here. It's beautiful!"

Daniel told her a group of girls and guys were going canoeing and camping and invited her to come along. They were leaving at 4:00 pm as it took a few hours to get to the campsite. Meaghan was about to explode with joy! She was going to make some friends at last. She got more and more excited as Daniel answered her many questions about what to bring and what happened on the trips. While walking back to the school, she started to realize there was a special connection between her and Daniel, and she was definitely intrigued.

In all the excitement, she did not realize how much time had passed. Meaghan had missed her English class with the debate team teacher. She went to the library for her free period, where she worried and wondered about the punishment for skipping class—something she had never done before. Her teacher came in and sat down across from her. He had a proposal for Meaghan: he wouldn't notify the school's office of her absence if she decided to join the debate club. If she still declined, she would serve a detention after school and her parents would be notified.

Choice A: _____

Choice B: _____

Choice C: _____

Consequence A: _____

Consequence B: _____

Consequence C: _____

Decision: _____

> *"The self is not something ready-made, but something in continuous formation through choice of action."*
> –John Dewey

smile inside

Deserted Island

Participants will work with a series of partners, modifying their opinions as they collect new information. They will compromise in order to reach an agreement.

materials   journals or paper, pens

1. Tell the participants to list the top ten things they would have to have if they were stranded alone on a deserted island. Have them keep the following in mind:

   - There are trees, bushes with berries, and fresh water on the island.
   - They must be able to carry the items.
   - Their decisions should be based on survival as rescue is not guaranteed.
   - They may want to include items to support their mental health.

2. In five-minute segments, have participants work with different partners to come up with new and improved lists. The goal is to agree on their combined top ten, but they may need to compromise.

3. After working with up to four different partners, allow everyone time to modify their original top ten lists from the knowledge and ideas they have gained.

4. Ask the group:

   - Did you find that listening to other's ideas proved to be good research?
   - Was it hard for anyone to change their original list? Why?
   - Is your modified list much different from your original list?
   - What items did you discard from your original list? Why?
   - What items did you add to your final list that weren't on your original list? Why?
   - What things did you realize you wouldn't want to live without?
   - Was it easy or difficult to defend your choices to others?
   - Why did we do this activity?
   - What did you learn from this activity?

5. Have a few participants share their modified lists aloud.

"Our very survival depends on our ability to stay awake, to adjust to new ideas, to remain vigilant, and to face the challenge of change."

—Martin Luther King Jr.

What to Do?

Participants will analyze a story with a moral dilemma and reach a group consensus on what the characters should do. They will discuss and reflect on other moral dilemmas.

materials   a *Dilemma* handout for each group of four, a visual aid, journals or paper, pens, a hat

1. Have participants take notes and ask the group:

   - What are values? (One's judgement of what is important in life.)
   - What are morals? (Standards of behavior decided by one's conscience; rules you set for yourself to guide decision making based on what you believe is right and wrong.)
   - How are the two related? (One's conscience makes decisions according to how one's values are prioritized. Basically, our values guide our moral decisions. When we change our values or belief systems, we change the way we morally respond to situations and life in general.)

2. Ask participants to get into groups of four. Give a *Dilemma* handout to each group.

3. Ask each group to read the dilemma, discuss it, and reach a consensus on what to do.

4. After each group shares, ask if everyone in the group fully agreed with the final decision. Ask the individuals who did not agree to state why.

5. Give everyone one of the following questions to respond to in their journals. Ask them to explain under what circumstances their answers would be "yes" and when they would be "no."

   - Would you lie for your boss if your job depended on it?
   - Would you steal something valuable to save someone's life?
   - Would you report someone you knew for vandalizing property?
   - Would you die to ensure your country's freedom?
   - Would you be willing to harm others for the sake of your loved ones?

6. Ask participants to write down moral dilemmas (from experience or hypothetical) for their peers to discuss. Put all of the dilemmas in a hat. Have each participant pick one and give their response.

"Compassion is the basis for all morality."

—Arthur Schonpenhauer

A Father's Dilemma

Vinnie, a hardworking, single father tried his best to raise his only child, Elisa. Elisa's alcoholic mother walked out when she was seven years old. Since then, Elisa's social and academic problems at school increased. All the teachers she worked with threw their hands up in frustration, unable to discipline her. She was reprimanded, given detentions, suspended, and finally expelled from school. Elisa showed no signs of cooperating.

Vinnie was worried his daughter would never receive a proper education. He thought she might do better at a boarding school in a neighboring state, where there was a very strict schedule and freedoms on campus had to be earned. So Vinnie enrolled his daughter when she turned fourteen. Due to the expensive tuition, he had to take a second job and work overtime. He didn't mind working day and night, for he loved his daughter very much and only wanted what was best for her.

Elisa seemed to do better in school and, up until a few weeks after her sixteenth birthday, there was no trouble. Vinnie received a call that completely devastated him. Elisa and three classmates at the boarding school were caught burglarizing a house in a local neighborhood. In juvenile court a judge found her guilty of breaking and entering and robbery. Elisa had been involved in this ring for almost two years.

The court costs and fines put Vinnie into debt. Elisa was sent to a juvenile detention home for eighteen months. When she returned home, she promised her father she would finish school and get a job to pay him back. At age eighteen, Elisa started eleventh grade at a public secondary school and spent her evenings working at a fast food restaurant.

A few months passed and all seemed well. At least Vinnie thought so. They never spent any time together since they were both always working. Then Vinnie got another upsetting call just as he was closing up the restaurant he managed. Elisa was in jail for possession of heroin. She had been using drugs and lying to him about everything.

Vinnie talked to a lawyer the following day and found out the fees and fines could add up to nearly $4,500. If they aren't paid, Elisa could spend anywhere from six months to two years in jail. Coming up with the money would cause Vinnie to lose his house.

What should Vinnie do?   What should Elisa do?

smile inside

Jasmine's Dilemma

Jasmine and Patrick had been going out with each other since tenth grade. On Valentine's Day in twelfth grade the arguing began. Patrick had been pressuring Jasmine to have sex for months. All his friends were sexually active and he didn't think it was fair that he had to wait another year when he and Jasmine were going to get married anyway. However, she wasn't ready for such a big step in their relationship. She wanted to wait until they married, which they planned to do after graduation.

Patrick couldn't wait, and he had a plan to make Jasmine change her mind. His friend's older brother was having a party in his off-campus house near the local university. Patrick stole some alcohol from his father's liquor cabinet and invited Jasmine to go to the party with him and his friends. He figured the alcohol would loosen her up and make her want to sleep with him.

Jasmine had always been curious about what alcohol would do to her, so she tried some vodka with orange juice at the party. She started to feel funny after two glasses and was laughing hysterically after four. Patrick made her laugh so hard when he started chugging down an entire bottle that she started to hiccup uncontrollably. Soon Patrick was vomiting and Jasmine was feeling very sleepy. She climbed into the backseat of his car to lie down.

Jasmine awoke to birds chirping and the sun shining across the windshield. She found Patrick lying on top of her. Both of them were undressed.

A few weeks later, she found out she was pregnant. She felt like Patrick had violated her body and she had never hated someone so much in her life. She couldn't believe her own boyfriend had raped her. Patrick insisted Jasmine had wanted to sleep with him just as much as he'd wanted to that night and she was just trying to put the blame on him for the pregnancy.

Her parents are against abortion and want her to have the baby and marry Patrick. If she doesn't they will disown her—no negotiating. Jasmine wants nothing to do with Patrick but knows how serious her anti-abortion parents are about disowning her.

What should Jasmine do?   What should Patrick do?

smile inside

GOAL SETTING

We live on a planet where instant gratification is increasingly accessible. Young people cannot always expect everything to be handed to them on demand. They have to be reminded that reaching goals requires focus, patience, and hard work.

To be productive and have success in life, an individual must be able to make plans and have the motivation to persevere. *Form Your Future* (p. 108) has participants creating short-term and long-term goals for themselves, then breaking the goals down into smaller steps and making commitments to follow through. *The New Me* (p. 112) provides a template for each individual to make personal improvements in his or her habits and character.

Visualize It! (p. 115) gives participants practice with visualization, which can strengthen their will power to achieve their set goals. Someone who has the necessary skills and can say, "I know I can do this" will be confident to aim high when setting goals and successful in achieving them.

Form Your Future

Participants will set and make plans for short-term and long-term goals they want to achieve. They will evaluate their progress in one month's time.

materials   *Form Your Future* handouts, pens, *Write Down Your Goals!* poem (optional)

1. An optional introduction to this activity is to share *Write Down Your Goals!* by Al Argo.

2. Explain to the participants that they are about to do a goal-setting exercise. They must choose one short-term and one long-term goal that excites them.

3. Pass out the handouts.

4. Point out that in order to reach a goal successfully, it helps to break it down into steps to make it more manageable. People tend to avoid or procrastinate if something seems overwhelming.

5. Give special mention to the My Affirmations section on the handouts. Creating statements like *I am an incredible guitar player.* and *I now have confidence in my strumming and knowledge of major chords.* tricks the mind into believing in the outcome before the goal is accomplished. This helps one overcome doubts and in turn, become more motivated. Stating the desired result in the present tense gives the mind a chance to get used to the idea which can make the goal seem easier to attain.

6. Give participants enough time to finish the handouts.

7. Ask participants to find partners and share what goals they would like to reach. Explain that talking about their goals will help them feel more committed to working toward them.

8. Make copies of their plans and revisit them one month later to let everyone evaluate their progress. Alternatively, have the participants seal their plans in a self-addressed envelope to be mailed at a later date.

> "The child's philosophy is a true one.
> He does not despise the bubble because
> it burst; he immediately sets to work to
> blow another one."
>
> —J.J. Proctor

Write Down Your Goals!

If you don't write your goal down on paper,
Beware, it may try to be an escaper.
But when you do write your goal in your journal,
what you have done is planted a kernel.
And everyone, who knows anything knows,
that what a man reaps is what a man sows!
So write down your hopes and journal your goals
and press on through the highs and the lows.
Through the thick and through the thin,
if you never, never quit—eventually you win.
In every failure is a seed of success,
so keep trying, keep trying—
And you'll be the best.
Write down your goals
and surprise the rest.

—Al Argo

(Used with permission from Al Argo, personal and professional development expert, author, and speaker.)

smile inside

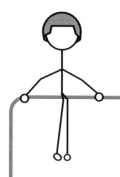

Form Your Future

A Short-Term Goal

What do I need to achieve this? _____

_____

_____

What steps do I have to take to meet all needs and reach my goal?

1. _____
2. _____
3. _____
4. _____
5. _____
6. _____
7. _____

My Commitments to Myself

I will _____

I will _____

I will _____

My Affirmations

I am _____

I now have _____

"As you think, so shall you become."
– Bruce Lee

smile inside

Form Your Future

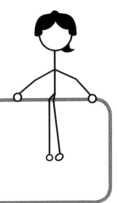

A Long-Term Goal

What do I need to achieve this? _____

_____

_____

What steps do I have to take to meet all needs and reach my goal?

1. _____
2. _____
3. _____
4. _____
5. _____
6. _____
7. _____

My Commitments to Myself

I will _____

I will _____

I will _____

My Affirmations

I am _____

I now have _____

"Success is not a destination…it is a journey. Thus the point you are at isn't nearly as important as the direction in which you are travelling."
—Author Unknown

smile inside

The New Me

Participants will identify behaviors they wish to change in themselves. They will analyze their behaviors, make plans and implement changes in their lives.

materials   *The New Me* handouts, pens

1. Explain to participants that this activity is about identifying a behavior of their own they want to improve. It can be the way they relate to others, a bad habit they would like to stop, or something they know will help them be happier or more successful but have had difficulty improving in the past.

2. Let participants know that in order to recognize an undesirable behavior one must be completely honest with oneself. Maintain that this is a confidential activity and their answers do not have to be shared with their peers.

3. Pass out the handouts and guide the group members as they fill in their answers.

4. When they begin to outline their plan, tell them to KISS—Keep It Simple, Silly! Simplifying something that seems difficult into small, achievable steps will make the goal easier to attain. Over time, a number of small steps will lead to the desired change.

5. Make copies of their statements and revisit them one month later to let everyone evaluate their progress. Alternatively, have them seal the handouts in a self-addressed envelope to be mailed at a later date.

"Happiness is not something ready made.
It comes from your own actions."

—The Dalai Lama XIV

The New Me

What's holding me back when it comes to being happier or more successful in my life?

_____

_____

What bad habits do I have that could be improved upon?

_____

_____

Is there anything about the way I relate to others that could be improved upon? What is it and how could it change?

_____

_____

After reflecting on the above answers, I have decided this is the change I wish to make in myself:

_____

_____

Why do I desire this change?

_____

_____

If I could see me and my new behavior on a movie screen, what would I see myself doing?

_____

_____

How will this new behavior make me feel?

_____

_____

What obstacles may slow my progress or prevent me from reaching my goal? What are they?

_____

_____

How can I overcome these obstacles?

_____

_____

What fears do I have to overcome to reach my goal?

What can I say to convince myself that this change is what I really want?

What beliefs do I have to change ?

How can I think differently?

What steps do I have to take to make this change in me?

What might my family, teachers, friends, or coach say to me after I have achieved my goal?

Is there anything I can do to maintain the new me?

My Commitments to Myself

I will

I will

I will

My Affirmations

I am

I now have

smile inside

Visualize It!

Participants will use affirmative statements and a visualization technique to assist them in implementing personal improvement in their lives.

materials   prepared affirmations, relaxing music, music player

> *Visualize It!* is best used in conjunction with
> *Form Your Future* (p. 108) or *The New Me* (p. 112).

1. Ask if anyone has ever heard of hypnosis being used as a tool for self-improvement (e.g., breaking bad habits, overcoming fears). Explain that in order to engage in self-improvement effectively, it's important to be relaxed and open to suggestion. The participants will be making suggestions to themselves, so in a way they will be using a form of self-hypnosis.

2. Explain that this activity will help everyone reach their personal improvement goals by using visualization as a tool. They can use the goals they set for themselves and their affirmations from *Form Your Future* (pp. 110-111) or *The New Me* (pp. 113-114). If the participants did not complete these handouts, then ask them to come up with one thing they would like to improve in themselves. They will need to create an affirmative statement that supports the change (e.g., someone who wants to be more confident could use *I am confident.* or *I now have confidence.*; someone who wants to stay out of trouble could use *I am responsible.*).

3. This is an internal exercise done in silence within the mind. Tell them the key to visualizing is to imagine what the scene would look like, similar to experiencing a memory.

4. Ask the participants to lie on their backs, play soothing music, and use the deep relaxation technique on page 116 to help everyone relax their bodies and clear their minds.

5. Lead them through the visualization exercise by reading pages 116-117 in a slow, soft voice.

6. Give the participants a minute to reorient themselves to the room. Have them share their experiences with the people closest to them. Ask if anyone would like to share anything from their visualization with the group. Reflect on their experiences.

7. Let participants know that any time they feel nervous about doing something, they can relax their bodies, clear their minds, and imagine themselves having success. Advise that this is a great exercise to do the night before a presentation, test, performance, or game.

"What the mind of man can conceive and believe, it can achieve."

—Author Unknown

Deep Relaxation

Begin by closing your eyes and breathing in deeply through your nose and out through your mouth. Take a couple of deep breaths to get fresh air circulating throughout your body. Take no notice of anyone else; we're all doing the same thing. This is your own personal time-out. Use it to relax.

(Pause.)

Now close your mouth and breathe just through your nose. Focus only on your breathing. Let's start by extending your breath. On your next inhale I'm going to count to four, pause, and then have you exhale to a count of eight. Ready? Breathing in, 1, 2, 3, 4… and breathing out, 1, 2, 3, 4, 5, 6, 7, 8. Inhale…1, 2, 3, 4… hold your breath for a moment and now exhale very slowly… 1, 2, 3, 4, 5, 6, 7, 8…

(Repeat once more and then go up to counts of 5/10 and 6/12.)

Now breathe at your own pace.

(Pause.)

With every breath in, let peaceful silence enter your mind. With every breath out, let go of any self-talk. Imagine all thoughts, worries, and distractions exiting your mind and leaving with your breath. Breathe in peaceful silence. Breathe out all thoughts. Do this a few times on your own.

(Pause.)

As your mind becomes clearer, allow your breathing to become more and more relaxed. I want you to begin to breathe in a way that is comfortable for you.

(Pause.)

Breathe in and tighten your feet (while pointing your toes). Hold your breath and stay tense…

(Pause for five seconds.)

Now release and slowly exhale. Feel the tension exiting your body, draining right out the soles of your feet.

(Pause for ten seconds. Repeat this step replacing "feet" with calves (while flexing your feet), thighs, hips and backside, stomach and lower back, chest and upper back, hands (clench your fists) and arms [tension now exits at the fingertips], shoulders and neck, and face and head.

Soften your forehead… your eyes… your jaw… your tongue. Just allow your body to remain in this state of complete relaxation. Breathe in… Breathe out.

(Pause for a few minutes.)

CONTINUE ON TO THE VISUALIZATION BELOW OR CONCLUDE THE DEEP RELAXATION WITH:

When you feel ready, open your eyes and begin to move your fingers and toes.

(Pause.)

Roll slowly to your left side. Help yourself up with your hands. Stay still and quiet. Remember this feeling of relaxation. Repeat this exercise anytime you're feeling stressed out.

Visualization

Imagine yourself in a beautiful meadow with green grass and purple and yellow wildflowers. The sky above is blue and the sun is shining gently.

(Pause.)

You see a massive tree in the meadow. Go to it.

(Pause.)

Now touch the rough texture of its bark.

(Pause.)

You hear the sound of a river flowing nearby. Move toward the sound of the water.

(Pause.)

smile inside

As you get closer, the sound gets louder. Once you reach the river, put your feet in the cool, moving water.
(Pause.)
Look down the river. You notice a wooden bridge arching over it. Go to the foot of the bridge.
(Pause.)
Look across the bridge. Reaching the other side represents becoming the new you. Picture yourself on the other side of the bridge, doing the things you will be doing with your new skill, behavior or attitude. What kind of situation do you see yourself in?
(Pause.)
What are you doing?
(Pause.)
Take a few steps onto the bridge.
(Pause.)
What kinds of things are you saying?
(Pause.)
How are you acting?
(Pause.)
Walk to the center of the bridge and look over the side at the water flowing underneath.
(Pause.)
Think of any fears, doubts, or worries you may have about making this change in yourself. Each time you think of one, imagine it as a stone. Throw it over the side of the bridge into the water and know that you're letting those fears, doubts, and worries go.
(Long pause.)
Imagine one last stone in your hand. Let this stone represent any remaining concerns that could possibly hold you back. Throw the stone into the river and turn toward the new you who is waiting on the other side of the bridge.
(Pause.)
Now there's nothing holding you back from making this change in yourself. Remember your affirmation.
(Pause.)
Say it in your mind with every step you take toward the new you.
(Pause.)
When you reach the end of the bridge, step into the new you.
(Long pause.)
Practice being the new you. How does it feel?
(Pause.)
What are you doing?
(Pause.)
What kinds of things are you saying?
(Pause.)
How are you acting?
(Long pause.)
I'm going to count to five and as I do, I would like you to take five deep, energizing breaths.
One… Two… each breath fills you with energy… Three… Four… Say your affirmation one more time… believing every word… Five… Bring your awareness and the new you back to the room. Wiggle your fingers and toes and slowly help yourself up with your hands.

GROUP DYNAMICS

Being able to work well with others is a vital ability. Individuals with the right skills and attitude can help turn any group experience into a success. On the contrary, individuals who are egocentric, righteous, or indolent can cause a group to fail. These negative attributes can be replaced by positive ones when identified with objectivity, humor, and concern for the best interest of everyone involved.

In this module, the mechanics of group work is observed. A better understanding of how certain behaviors affect the progress of the group will enable the participants to increase their effectiveness when working as part of a team.

In *Keep It Going!* (p. 120) and *Lap Sit* (p. 121), the participants practice methods to improve group success and learn to revise strategies when collaborating. *Xs and Os* (p. 122) and *Obey the Crown* (p. 124) expose the barriers that prevent group cohesiveness, such as competitive attitudes and blocking behaviors.

If someone's instructions are not followed or a message is not relayed properly, the results of a project could be less than desired. *Trust Walk* (p. 123) and *Peanut Butter and Banana Sandwich* (p. 129) promote building trust with others, following instructions, and learning the importance of effective communication.

Another part of understanding group dynamics is stepping back and recognizing the diverse roles one can play in a group, which takes place throughout *Observe and Tally* (p. 126). During *Rate It!* (p. 130), everyone learns how to improve a group's ability to function by identifying mistakes and weaknesses as well as evaluating what does work in order to improve productivity. Finally, different leadership styles are experienced and evaluated in *Follow the Leader* (p. 132).

All the activities in this module enhance cooperation and prepare participants for future group work in the Esprit de Corps through Service Learning module. The project work they undertake will require every individual to be accountable for his or her learning, communication, participation, and attitude.

Keep It Going!

Participants will work as a group to improve their performance during a challenging task. They will set targets and discuss ways to improve their strategies. They will evaluate their progress and decide which decisions brought them higher degrees of success.

30 min

materials   one tennis ball per participant, flat area for bouncing balls, stopwatch for each group

1. Begin the activity by having groups of five to six participants stand in a circle with one person holding one ball.

2. Have the participants initiate a pattern of their choosing by bouncing the ball from person to person until everyone has handled the ball once. The last person will pass it back to the starting point.

3. Tell them to pass the ball to the same person each time. Add another ball to follow the path of the first.

4. Have them all stop and ask the groups how many balls they think they can keep going and for how long with success. After they've set themselves a target, request they do the first trial without speaking and time them. Give them their results.

5. Have the groups identify ways they could improve their strategy (e.g., change the diameter of the circle, pay attention to the angle of the bounce, use both hands, all pass at the same time). After the discussion, time them again and allow open communication during the process. Give them their results.

6. Have the group members measure their success by asking the following:

   - Did you meet your target?
   - If yes, what enabled you to get there?
   - If no, what prevented you from reaching it?
   - How did you feel when you were not allowed to communicate?

7. For a further challenge, ask the group to synchronize a ball pass to the right. Everyone must stand in a circle and each person must have a ball. Most likely, the group will try to bounce the balls which makes it difficult. Allow time for trial and error and then emphasize the word, "pass." The best option for success is to stand close with the balls in their right hands and gently toss to the right at the same time.

8. Analyze the success of the challenge once the goal is reached. Ask the group:

   - What helped you succeed?
   - What lessons about teamwork can we learn from this experiment? (Communication is crucial, planning an effective strategy is important, trial and error can help improve strategy, be open to exploring new ways of doing things, etc.)

9. Alternatively, break the participants up into small groups and have them compete against each other. Each group can be timed separately or simultaneously to see how long they can keep five tennis balls in motion without dropping any.

    smile inside

Lap Sit

Participants will work together to achieve a goal.

materials   carpeted or grassy area

1. This activity works best if participants of similar heights are next to each other. Ask them to line up with the tallest in the middle and the shortest on both ends. Have the ends of the lines meet to make a shoulder to shoulder circle clear of any objects.

2. Give the following instructions:

    - Turn to your left so that you face the back of the person next to you.
    - Take a sideways step toward the center of the circle. Look around to make sure the group is still in a perfect circle.
    - Take another small step in and another until the circle is very tight.
    - Be sure the circle is perfectly round and there are no gaps.
    - On the count of three, slowly sit down on the lap of the person behind you. One, two, three, sit.

3. Once they are successful, have the group members all stand on the count of three to prevent everyone from falling in a heap.

4. During a sturdy and successful lap sit, the group can attempt various tricks:

    - No hands
    - Sway back and forth
    - Walk in a circle, to the left, and to the right

5. Ask the group:

    - What went well?
    - What went wrong?
    - What could have improved your performance as a group?
    - What would you do differently if you did another lap sit?

6. Have the group attempt another lap sit if there are suggestions for improved performance or a challenge.

7. Alternatively, put the participants in multiple groups and challenge each group to remain in a strong lap sit for the longest period of time. Groups that fall down must stay down.

8. Process the experience by asking, "What did you learn about teamwork from this activity?"

Xs & Os

Participants will play a game that, unbeknownst to them, requires cooperation. They will process their behaviors in hindsight. They will discuss how competition is embedded in society and how it can affect behavior.

materials   a visual aid

1. Draw a grid of six squares by six squares on the visual aid.

2. Split the group into teams to represent Xs and Os.

3. Say to the group, "the object of the game is to create a line of Xs and Os on the grid."

4. Allow alternating team members to come forth to place their marks on the grid—one from team X, one from team O and so on.

5. Once the grid is full of Xs and Os, examine it with the teams. More than likely the teams will have blocked each other from creating a line.

6. Ask the teams, "Why did you keep blocking each other?" Process what just happened with the teams (they automatically assumed they were to stop the other group from achieving the goal). Repeat the instructions of the game just as before to prove the point.

7. Ask the group:

   • Why do you think you assumed it was a competition?
   • How is competition embedded in society?
   • How does this affect the behavior of people in general?

8. Encourage them to think *How can we all work together so everyone wins?* instead of *How can I win?* when approaching group situations.

> "*Tell me, I forget.*
> *Show me, I remember.*
> *Involve me, I understand.*"
>
> —Confucius

smile inside

Trust Walk

Participants will act as leaders and followers in a trust walk. They will discuss their feelings associated with trust in group work.

materials   a rope for each group (optional), blindfolds for each participant (optional)

1. Ask the participants to form groups of four. Chose individuals who are well-spoken and honest to lead first in each group. The other group members can wear blindfolds and all hold onto a rope in a single file line or simply close their eyes and put a hand on the shoulder of the person in front of them.

2. The leader of each group is responsible for leading their group around (preferably outdoors) safely. They must walk slowly and warn the others of upcoming obstacles:

   - We're stepping up onto a grassy area!
   - We're circling a tree stump. Walk in a circle to your left.
   - Be careful of the pavement, it's slippery.

3. Emphasize to the leader it's their responsibility to ensure each individual's safety.

4. Tell those who are blindfolded they must do their best to trust the leader completely.

5. After a few minutes, ask the leaders of each group to go to the end and let the next in line take their place. Continue until everyone has had a chance to be the leader.

6. Discuss the feelings that arose in each individual. Ask the group:

   - Was it difficult to have complete trust in the leader?
   - Did you trust one leader more than another? Why?
   - Who had to peek? Why?
   - Was anyone afraid of getting hurt?
   - Did it get easier as you went along?
   - In what other kinds of situations do we have to trust people?
   - How does trust come into play when you're doing a project with a group?
   - Why is trust important in group situations?
   - What do you need from someone in order to trust them?
   - What can you do to help others trust you?

7. Alternatively, this activity can be done in pairs with an indoor obstacle course.

Obey the Crown

Participants will obey commands that slow group progress while carrying out a task. They will discuss barriers that negate or prevent success when working in groups.

materials   *Obey the Crown Commands* and masking tape or party hats with labels affixed, paper and pens

1. Prepare a set of "crowns" for each group of six members. Distribute them by either sticking a card to each participant's forehead or place a party hat on their head without letting anyone see their own label.

2. Explain to the participants that they must obey the commands displayed on their group members' labels throughout the task.

3. Assign a simple task to the groups such as rank the top five fast-food restaurants, TV shows, or superheroes.

4. Tell the groups they must come to a consensus. If they seem to be making any real progress, remind the participants to continue to obey the commands. Monitor the groups during this hilarious, but frustrating and often noisy task.

5. Stop the activity after about five minutes and have the participants guess what is written on their "crowns."

6. Conduct a follow-up discussion with everyone. Ask the group:

   - Who guessed what was written on your crown?
   - How did it feel to be treated that way?
   - What were your frustrations during this task?
   - Who made the task the most difficult to complete?
   - Do you think people unknowingly invite others to treat them in a certain way? How?
   - Do you think someone's reputation can have an effect on how people treat them? What can one do to change that?
   - What prevented your group's success?
   - What other barriers might prevent a group's success? (Poor communication, apathy, conflict, etc.)
   - Has anyone experienced being treated like this before in a group situation? What happened and how did you deal with it?

7. Ask everyone to take a moment to say something kind to the people in the group who were treated poorly during the activity. Remind the participants it generally takes about three good experiences to make up for a bad one in the real world.

8. Collect the crowns and have the groups complete their tasks without any barriers.

9. Ask the group:

   - How did the group dynamics change when this task was done without the labels?
   - When is it beneficial to treat someone a particular way in a group? (When there are appointed roles.)
   - What did you learn from doing this activity?

smile inside

Agree with me	Disagree with me
Put me in charge	Argue with me
Laugh at what I say	Flirt with me
Make me take notes	Ignore me
Stare at my nose	Ask me to speak up
Interrupt me	Compliment me

Observe & Tally

Participants will learn about common roles in groups. They will decide what roles they tend to play in group settings and analyze the roles their peers play. They will reevaluate their participation in a group after listening to their peers' observations.

materials   a visual aid, journals or paper, pens, *Tally Sheet* handouts

1. Write the following nine common roles in groups on the visual aid without the definitions:

    (Initiator)   gives ideas for procedure, keeps the group on task

    (Organizer)   puts ideas into writing, leads the group to completion

    (Evaluator)   brings common points of view to the group's attention, draws conclusions, summarizes the consensus of the group

    (Seeker)   asks others for information and opinions, asks questions, finds needed information through research

    (Informer)   gives information and opinions, answers questions

    (Mediator)   gives solutions to conflicts, helps with compromises, analyzes what's impeding progress, interjects humor to relieve tension

    (Encourager)   gives praise, makes positive comments, draws out the shy ones in the group

    (Follower)   acts as an audience member to the discussion, is agreeable

    (Blocker)   argues nonsensically, tells stories, competes for attention, displays unusual behavior, gets off task, does not participate, slows or prevents group progress

2. Ask the participants what responsibilities each role might take on or what behaviors they might display during a group project. Integrate their suggestions and write revised definitions on the visual aid. Have them take notes.

3. Have the participants write down which roles they think they tend to play in groups in their journals.

4. Divide participants into groups of six. Tell the members of each group to act naturally and give them a hypothetical task such as:

    * Plan a dance. Come up with a theme, colors, refreshments, entertainment, and decorations. Make a to-do list and delegate tasks.
    * Plan a fundraiser for a local charity. Decide on a charity, what kind of event and how it will make money. Make a to-do list and delegate tasks.

smile inside

5. Pass out a *Tally Sheet* handout to every participant. Instruct group members to take turns standing outside of their group to silently observe the dynamics. Each time the observer catches someone displaying a characteristic of a particular role, he or she is to put a tally mark under the person's name in the appropriate row.

6. Rotate observers in and out of the groups by tapping their shoulders or by setting a time limit. Stop the task after all participants have had a chance to observe.

7. Have the observers total the tally marks and share with each other the roles they played. Give them some time to discuss the behavior of the members of their groups.

8. Ask everyone to respond to the following questions in their journals:

   - Which role did the observers say you played the most? Did this surprise you? Why? Or did it match your guess before the activity? How did you predict this?
   - Which role would you like to master the most? Why?
   - Which role do you think you would be the best at given practice? Why?
   - What skills and characteristics do you need to cultivate in order to improve in your chosen role?
   - Which roles would you like to avoid if at all possible? Why?

"*There are three kinds of people:
those who make things happen,
those who watch things happen,
and those who wonder what happened.*"

—Nicholas Butler Murray

smile inside

Tally Sheet

Names:						
Initiator						
Organizer						
Evaluator						
Seeker						
Informer						
Mediator						
Encourager						
Follower						
Blocker						

"The important thing is this:
to be able at any moment to sacrifice
what we are for what we could become."

– Charles DeBois

smile inside

Peanut Butter & Banana Sandwich

Participants will write instructions and watch how literally they're interpreted.
They will give accurate verbal instructions to ensure success.

materials   paper, pens, a jar of peanut butter, a few bananas, a loaf of bread, butter knives, a visual aid

1. Ask everyone to write out instructions on how to make a peanut butter and banana sandwich.

2. Choose the most entertaining instructions to read and follow them exactly. For example:

   - *Put the peanut butter on one slice and banana on another. Put together and eat.*
     (Put the jar of peanut butter on a slice of bread and an unpeeled banana on another.
     Stack the awkward sandwich and jokingly attempt to bite into it.)

   - *Put the peanut butter and banana on and enjoy your sandwich.*
     (Spread the peanut butter on your hand, put the banana on your head, and smile at
     two pieces of plain bread.)

   - *Put banana on bread. Spread the peanut butter on the banana. Put the bread on top.*
     (Place a banana on the loaf of bread. Spread the peanut butter with your finger on
     the skin of a banana and turn it all upside down.)

3. Ask the group:

   - What point am I trying to make? (It's important to be clear when giving instructions, you can't assume
     that others will understand something, etc.)
   - Has anyone ever encountered problems with miscommunication on a project? With friends or
     family? What happened?
   - Why is accurate communication so important? (Because things can go wrong, feelings can get hurt,
     people can get lost, etc.)
   - What helps make communication clear? (Precise explanations, a commitment of time, avoiding
     assumptions, opportunities to check for understanding, etc.)

4. Ask the group to provide explicit instructions for making a peanut butter and banana sandwich.
   Have one volunteer write them on the visual aid while a few volunteers (who have washed their hands)
   demonstrate.

5. Invite everyone to taste a properly made peanut butter and banana sandwich.

smile inside

Rate It!

Participants will evaluate their group's performance. They will identify the group's strengths and weaknesses and make plans to improve their group's success.

materials   journals or paper, pens

To maximize cooperation, it's best to process after group project sessions. Use *Rate It!* after the group sessions during the *Make a Change Challenge* (p. 150).

1. Have the group members write the following definition in their journals:

   (Group processing)

   When a group reviews an experience and decides what went well and not so well. This reflection time allows the group to make plans to do things differently in the future to improve its effectiveness. Group processing can also prevent conflict amongst the group members by addressing problems as they come up instead of waiting until things are beyond repair.

2. Explain that consistent group processing reminds us to compliment group members, evaluate progress and suggest ideas for future success. It provides an opportunity for group members to tactfully communicate their feelings to prevent frustrations from turning into resentment or unproductive behaviour. One of the most valuable lessons to learn about group dynamics is that we cannot change others, only how we react to challenging behaviors and situations. When a behavior irritates us, we can use the experience as a personal growth opportunity to make sure we are not doing the same things to others.

3. The following are ideas for group processing activities:

   - Rate your group experience from one to five stars and explain why you gave it that rating.
   - Compliment deserving group members for their work.
   - Assess your progress and make plans for the next session.
   - Anonymously write one positive and one negative thing about how the group is performing on slips of paper. Nominate one person to read them aloud and then, as a group, discuss how to resolve the negative issues.
   - Share a personal strength and a weakness with your group. Discuss how you plan to improve or diversify your contribution to the group.
   - Request a third party for a mediation session if there are complicated issues in your group.
   - Openly discuss or respond in writing to one or more of the processing questions.

4. The following are processing questions to choose from:

   - What went well in your group today?
   - What could have gone better in your group today?
   - Were there any behaviors that held the group back today? What were they? Have you ever acted similarly? Why might someone act that way?
   - What did you learn about working with others today?

smile inside

- What could you do differently next time to help improve your group's productivity?
- Did your group have any valuable learning experiences today? What were they?
- What would improve your group's cooperation?
- Was everyone cooperative during this session? Who was not and why?
- Did everyone contribute equally today? If no, why not?
- Did everyone have the chance to express their opinions today? If no, why not?
- What were the group's successes today? Failures?
- What is a problem in your group? What caused it? How can it be resolved?
- Who came up with a good idea? What was it?
- What role(s) did you (or others) play today? (See *Observe and Tally*, p. 126) What were your responsibilities?
- Who in your group would you like to compliment and why?
- Is there anything you would have done differently today if you were to do it over again?
- If you had a lot more time, what would you want to do to make the project even better?
- Who was the most positive during this session? What did they do or say?
- Did you notice any negativity during today's session? If yes, why did this occur?
- What personal realizations did you have about your own behavior or attitude after this group experience?

*"Obstacles are those frightful things you see
when you take your eyes off your goal."*

—Henry Ford

Follow the Leader

Participants will create group sculptures with leaders who secretly represent the following: a dictator, a laissez-faire leader, and a democratic leader. The groups will present their sculptures and discuss their experiences under the different leadership styles.

60 min

materials   the same amount of construction materials for each group: popsicle sticks, straws, glue, tape, scissors, paper, cardboard, markers, etc.

1. There needs to be at least three groups of four to six participants for this activity to work optimally. Have each group choose their leader.

2. Privately assign one of the following roles to the group leaders:

   (Dictator   )

   Give orders about how the job will get done. Make sure the sculpture is a product of your ideas. Do not use any group member's suggestions.

   (Democratic leader   )

   Work with the group members and use their suggestions throughout the project. Involve every one and use consensus to make decisions. Delegate responsibilities fairly.

   (Laissez-faire leader   )

   Do not give any suggestions on how to organize the group. Let everyone do what they want to do. Make sure the sculpture is a product of their ideas only.

3. Explain that their task is to create sculptures that represent how a group should work together or allow all the groups to decide their own themes. They must listen to their leaders and finish within thirty minutes.

4. When time has expired, representatives from each group, excluding the leaders, should present their final products and explain the meanings behind all the parts of their sculptures.

5. After each presentation, ask the group members to share how their leader acted. Ask each leader to share the leadership style he or she represented.

6. Conduct a secret ballot vote to choose the best sculpture and reveal the winner.

7. Ask the group:

   * How did it feel to work under your leader?
   * What are the advantages and disadvantages of each style of leadership?
   * Can you name a situation that's perfect for each style of leadership? (E.g., Dictator: on a construction site. Democratic leader: a meeting organizing the design of a new community center. Laissez-faire leader: any situation where creativity needs to flourish.)
   * Did you vote for your own sculpture? Who didn't? (Most likely those under a dictator did not because they didn't feel ownership of their sculpture. Draw this conclusion with the class.)

    smile inside

Everybody, Somebody, Anybody, and Nobody

This is a little story about four people named
Everybody, Somebody, Anybody, and Nobody.

There was an important job to do and
Everybody was asked to do it.

Everybody was sure that Somebody would do it.

Anybody could have done it, but Nobody did it.

Somebody got angry because it was Everybody's job.

Everybody thought that Anybody could do it,
but Nobody realized that Everybody wouldn't do it.

It ended up that Everybody blamed Somebody
when Nobody did what Anybody could have done.

Author Unknown

(adapted from *The Responsibility Poem* by Charles Osgood)

This module promotes harmonious teamwork and civic engagement. The participants apply the skills they have practiced in previous modules in order to create a positive group experience when members work well together toward a common goal.

It is important that the activities within this module are completed sequentially in order to best prepare participants for service learning in *Make a Change Challenge* (p. 150). They will decide on a social issue they are passionate about and then influence that area in a positive way.

The module is facilitated using inquiry-based methods and the participants are responsible for:

- Exploring options.
- Determining directions.
- Planning projects.
- Asking the right questions.
- Discovering information and resources.
- Organizing findings.
- Making conclusions.
- Testing ideas.
- Managing time.
- Reporting contributions.
- Presenting projects.

The inquiry-based learning method is beneficial because it forces participants to search their minds for where information is lacking and then organize what they encounter into the constructs of their thinking. They learn how to ask the right questions through trial and error, which facilitates their comprehension. They are challenged to be flexible and overcome anxieties related to approaching others and public speaking. The module is semi-structured so participants can learn from the mistakes they make, which serves to reinforce learning.

Although there are often time constraints when working with young people, giving them as much time as possible to work on their projects reaps the greatest benefits for both the participants and the community. The skills and confidence gained from carrying out service-learning projects strengthen the participants' beliefs in their abilities to achieve. The intrinsic rewards positively influence self-respect and a sense of purpose in their lives.

An optional but relevant introduction for this module is to watch the film *Pay It Forward* (2000). It runs for 119 minutes and is rated PG-13 due to adult themes and violence.

Mind Mapping

Participants will mind map issues that affect youth, schools, or the community. They will brainstorm ideas that will make a positive impact on a social problem.

materials   large sheets of paper, markers, journals or paper, pens

1. Mind map issues in the areas of youth, school, and/or community while the participants take notes in their journals. Alternatively, create three groups and assign the three topics. Have them create mind maps to share with everyone. See example below:

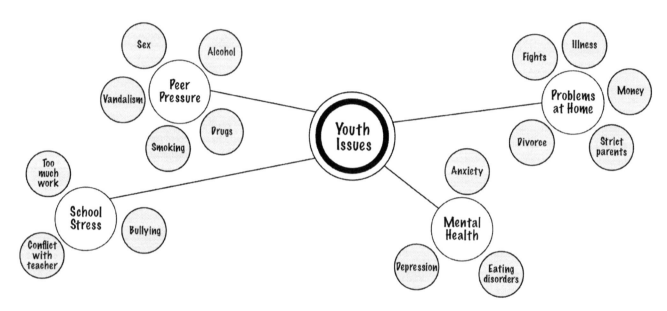

2. Pick an issue and conduct a brainstorming session with no rules. Ask the participants to come up with ideas that will have a positive impact on that issue or possible solutions. Encourage everyone to think big and be creative.

Examples of ideas for youth issues:
- Raise awareness about mental health issues by creating a display with information on how to get help.
- Distribute brochures to parents on how to understand teenagers to prevent family conflict.

Examples of ideas for school issues:
- To discourage littering, beautify the area outside the school by planting trees or flowers.
- Facilitate conflict resolution training to assist with problems during lunch.

Examples of ideas for community issues:
- Raise money to buy toys for the animal rescue shelter.
- Present ideas that will help with the graffiti problem to the city council.

3. Ask all participants to write their names next to the issues that interest them the most. Keep the mind maps to revisit if you do *Action Planning* (p. 138).

smile inside

The Longest List

Participants will brainstorm methods of communication in teams.

materials large sheets of paper, pens

1. Divide the participants into teams of at least five. Give the teams three minutes to brainstorm all the possible ways to communicate messages. Encourage teams to be as quick and original as they can. They will score a point for every answer that no other team has.

Possible answers:

- speaking
- writing
- singing
- poetry
- facial expressions
- body language
- paintings
- sign language
- sculpture
- dance
- music
- Morse code
- smoke signals
- billboards

- magazines
- books
- e-mails
- protests
- social media
- websites
- newspapers
- singing telegrams
- brochures
- business cards
- radio
- TV
- film
- commercials

- pantomime
- photos
- signs
- ads
- skywriting
- postcards
- posters
- phone calls
- text messages
- speeches
- petitions
- messages on clothing
- fax
- graffiti

2. Have a representative from each team take turns giving an answer from their list. They may not repeat an answer once it has been given.

3. Write all the answers on a large sheet of paper. Teams receive a point for each unique answer. The team with the most points wins the challenge.

4. Keep the final list. It will serve as a good reference for the *Make a Change Challenge* (p. 150) activity.

smile inside

Action Planning

Participants will outline the steps of an action plan for a hypothetical project.

materials   long strips of paper and sticky tack or AV equipment with a word processing program, journals or paper, pens, maps from *Mind Mapping* (p. 136)

1. If *Mind Mapping* has been completed, revisit one of the mind map issues. Otherwise, choose a social problem for this activity.

2. Without giving participants any direction, ask them to come up with a procedure that will see a hypothetical service project through from start to finish. The goal is to make a positive impact on a social issue.

3. Write each of the steps they give for the action plan procedure on separate strips of paper. Accept all suggestions as they go through the thought process and post the strips for all to see. Alternatively, use a word processing program and projector.

4. Guide participants toward a sequential, logical, and comprehensive list by asking questions about the hypothetical project. As participants come up with new actions, ask them to decide where they should be inserted in the procedure list.

5. Once the group is satisfied with their steps for the procedure, distribute the *Action Plan Steps* handouts so they can compare it to what they have. Allow them to revise their plan, if they wish, before recording the final procedure.

6. If you are proceeding with the activities in this module, ask the participants to have another look at the mind maps and start thinking about which topic interests them the most. Let them know the projects and groups will be decided at the beginning of the next session, *Organization 101* (p. 140).

"The difference between what we do and what we are capable of doing would suffice to solve most of the world's problems."

—Mahatma Gandhi

smile inside

Action Plan Steps

1. Choose an issue.
2. Brainstorm ideas.
3. Decide on a purpose.
4. Set a goal.
5. Research the issue.
   a) Search the Internet.
   b) Find out what's being done.
   c) Conduct a survey and analyze the data.
   d) Interview people who know about the topic.
6. Revise the goal.
7. Get permission.
8. Make a detailed plan.
   a) What has to be done?
   b) What is needed?
   c) Who can be recruited to help?
   d) How can the resources be gathered?
9. Create a timeline.
10. Assign tasks.
11. Carry out tasks.
12. Hold group processing sessions periodically.
13. Achieve the goal.
14. Evaluate the results.
15. Publicize the outcome.

Organization 101

20 min

Participants will use action plans, action logs and a calendar to stay organized throughout their *Make a Change Challenge* project. They will brainstorm ideas to help solve a problem.

materials   each group requires: a large envelope, one *Action Plan* handout, one *Action Log* handout, and *Calendar* handouts, journals or paper, pens

1. Have the participants choose topics and form groups for the upcoming *Make a Change Challenge* (p. 150).

2. Distribute the envelopes, *Action Plan* handouts, *Action Log* handouts, and *Calendar* handouts. Advise the groups to keep these pages in their envelopes throughout the project as well as all researched materials including names, phone numbers, photocopies, pages printed from the Internet, etc.

3. Go through the purpose of each handout with the groups.

    (Action Plan)

    The action plan facilitates project planning and keeps the group on track. Participants should fill out most of it over the next few sessions during the *What's Happening?* (p. 149) research period.

    (Action Log)

    The action log details individual contributions to the project. Each time a task is completed, the individual must record his or her efforts. This will help keep the workload evenly distributed.

    (Calendar)

    The calendar assists with time management. Participants can keep track of short-term goals and have an overview of the number of sessions they have left to work on the project.

4. Give the groups deadlines for the completion of their projects as well as the dates for their presentations. Suggest that the groups work backward from their goal if possible, using the calendar to create a timeline of their future activities.

5. Remind them to refer to the procedure list they came up with in *Action Planning* (p. 138).

6. Pressure the groups to do a power brainstorming session by only giving them ten minutes initially. Encourage them to write down every idea they come up with even if it seems far-fetched.

7. Each group will be unique, so it's important to be flexible in the facilitator role from this point on. When approached, ask questions instead of providing answers so the groups are forced to problem solve.

"Feel the power that comes from focusing on what excites you."

—Oprah

smile inside

Action Plan

Project Name:

Group members:

Issue of concern:

Possible solutions:

Can this problem be solved? What level of impact can we make?

What is our motivation? Our purpose?

OUR GOAL:

How does our goal help with this issue? Who does it help?

What will we have to do in order to achieve this goal?

smile inside

What do we know about this issue?

What do we want to know?

How can we find out what people being affected by this issue think?

Who can give us the information we need?

How else are we going to get information?

"The secret of getting ahead is getting started. The secret of getting started is breaking your complex, overwhelming tasks into small manageable tasks and then starting on the first one."

– Mark Twain

smile inside

How did we find out what people being affected by this issue think?

What do people being affected by this issue think?

What are its effects?

What are its causes?

What is presently being done to help with this issue?

What else have we discovered?

Revised Goal

What do we know now that we didn't know when we stated our goal?

Does this affect our original goal?

Do we want to make any changes to our goal now that we've done our research?
What are they and why are these changes important?

Do we want to make any changes to our original plan now that we've learned more?
What are they and why are these changes important?

Permission

Do we need permission from anyone to reach our goal? From whom?

How can we get it?

When and how did we get it?

How are we going to achieve our goal?

What do we need to achieve this goal?

Who can help us achieve our goal? What could they do?

What are the strengths of the members of our group?

Who is going to do what?

How are we going to measure the success of our project?

How did we measure the success of our project?

What are the results of the evaluation?

If we had a chance to do it all over, what would we do differently?

Discuss and reflect on the following statement: "Changing me changes the world; changing the world changes me."

> " Few will have the greatness to bend history itself; but each of us can
> work to change a small portion of events, and in the total of all those acts
> will be written the history of this generation."
>
> – Robert F. Kennedy

Action Log

PROJECT NAME _____

GROUP MEMBERS _____

TASK	TIME INVOLVED	DATE COMPLETED	SIGNATURE

"I have been impressed with the urgency of doing. Knowing is not enough; we must apply. Being willing is not enough; we must do."

– Leonardo da Vinci

"Today's preparation determines tomorrow's achievement."

SUNDAY	MONDAY	TUESDAY	WEDNESDAY	THURSDAY	FRIDAY	SATURDAY
SUNDAY	MONDAY	TUESDAY	WEDNESDAY	THURSDAY	FRIDAY	SATURDAY
SUNDAY	MONDAY	TUESDAY	WEDNESDAY	THURSDAY	FRIDAY	SATURDAY
SUNDAY	MONDAY	TUESDAY	WEDNESDAY	THURSDAY	FRIDAY	SATURDAY

What's Happening?

Participants will use a variety of research methods to educate themselves about social issues. They will present their findings to the rest of their group.

materials project envelopes with handouts, journals or paper, pens, Internet and library access, phone

1. Have the project groups that were formed during *Organization 101* (p. 140) meet to organize a *Research Plan* (p. 142) for their chosen social issue.

2. Insist that the groups investigate their issue thoroughly using a variety of methods and require them to delegate responsibilities in order to address all the questions on the *Research Results* handout (p. 143).

3. The groups may need to be reminded that setting up interviews, conducting surveys, and requesting information packets are priorities. Suggest they find out what approaches have failed and have had success in regards to affecting change with their issue.

4. Encourage the groups to be flexible with their original goal because they may have new insights after they carry out their research.

5. Reserve the second one-hour session for group members to report their findings to the rest of their group and record the research results in the action plans.

6. Hold the group members accountable for their contributions to the project by implementing one of the following research and report methods:

   He Said/She Said

   Two group members interview each other about the information they have independently researched. They must then orally present their partner's findings to the rest of their group.

   Puzzle

   Each group member reads a different section from the same article about the topic and then teaches the rest of the group what they have learned.

7. If this is just a one-off activity, invite guests from the community who are knowledgeable in the areas the participants are researching (e.g., a school psychologist, a representative from a local agency or non-profit organization) to answer the groups' questions.

"Never doubt that a small group of thoughtful, committed citizens can change the world. Indeed, it is the only thing that ever has."

—Margaret Mead

smile inside

Make a Change Challenge

Participants will finalize their goals and work together to carry out service-learning projects. They will be randomly interviewed about their group's progress. They will present the development and outcome of their projects with their peers.

materials project envelopes with handouts from *Organization 101* (p. 140), the list from *The Longest List* (p. 137), research findings from *What's Happening?* (p. 149), pens

1. Ideally, the duration of the entire project will be approximately thirty hours: three hours a week for ten weeks, but less ambitious projects can be successfully executed in under ten hours over three weeks.

2. After *Organization 101* and *What's Happening?*, let the groups work independently until the project is complete. Advise them to continually update their *Action Plans* and *Calendars* and to record every task, no matter how small, in their *Action Logs*.

3. If a group decided to send for information, conduct a survey, or interview people, ask them to wait to revise their goal until they have conducted all necessary research.

4. Remind groups who want to affect change by raising awareness about an issue or who are promoting an event to refer to *The Longest List* for inspiration.

5. Tell the groups that during different phases of the project, one individual will randomly be asked about his or her group's progress. This will encourage all group members to stay actively engaged.

6. Insist that groups report difficult problems and get permission when it's necessary.

7. Require all group members to take part in the final presentation of their projects. Ask them to tell the story of their group's journey from start to finish. Invite groups to enhance their presentations with photos and/or videos.

8. Acknowledge the participants for their efforts after the presentations with certificates of appreciation or wait until *Celebration Day* (p. 156). Visit www.smileinside.com.au to download a color version of the certificate.

"The best way to find yourself is to lose yourself in the service of others."

—Ralph Waldo Emerson

smile inside

Certificate of Appreciation

This award is presented to:

in acknowledgment of valuable contributions and remarkable achievements.

Signed:

Date:

smile inside

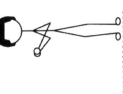
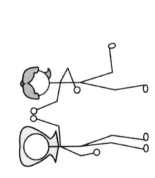

CULMINATION

A perfect way to bring the *Smile Inside* experience to a close is with reflective self-analyses as outlined in *Who Am I?* (p. 154). It is a beneficial and valuable exercise for the participants, but can also be very fulfilling for the facilitator as their words and insights give glimpses into the realizations they have had about themselves.

The activities within this module facilitate uplifting and meaningful experiences that will help the group bond on an emotional level. The activities can take place in their last few sessions together, just save one or two for *Celebration Day* (p. 156).

Concluding with *Celebration Day* will make your last day memorable. It can be organized as a ceremonial rite of passage over dinner or as a fun, casual party. Presenting certificates of appreciation for all of the participants' hard work during the *Make a Change Challenge* (p. 150) or recognizing individuals for personal achievements in front of their peers does wonders for their self-respect. If possible, set aside enough time on *Celebration Day* so they can write in each other's journals.

Who Will Be...? (p. 157) requires a bit of preparation but is significant for everyone involved. Group members are asked to predict their peers' futures by recalling their interests or making recommendations for their personality types.

Circle of Silence (p. 158) is challenging for most because looking into another's eyes for a stretch can be uncomfortable. If participants are able to move past that it can produce some remarkable encounters. The experience should be conducted with seriousness and sensitivity, allowing participants to make unaffected and genuine connections.

Playing the game of *Psychiatrist* (p. 159) is lot of fun and a great way to get everyone laughing. During *Symbolic Gifts* (p. 160) participants must recollect their time together to decide on a hypothetical perfect gift for every member of the group.

These memorable culminating activities can have a profound impact on the participants and are an enjoyable way to wrap things up.

Who Am I?

Participants will respond in writing to the question "Who am I?"

materials a visual aid or *Who Am I?* handouts, journals, paper, pens

1. This activity can be used as an assessment tool to measure their level of understanding of the concepts presented throughout the program or just as a final journal reflection.

2. Display the example below on a visual aid or pass out the *Who Am I?* handouts. Ask the participants to think deeply about the question "Who am I?" and write their response in their journals or on paper.

3. Set a time limit or have them complete the assignment at home.

4. Allow them to use their journals or notes from previous activities as references.

Who Am I?

This experience was meant to help you:

- discover your potential as an individual.
- explore your relationships with others.
- realize how you can make a difference in the world.

Think deeply about what you have discovered about yourself during our time together and respond to the question "Who am I?"

---

smile inside

Who Am I?

Reflect on the question, "Who am I?" and respond. It should be a written discussion of you at this point in your life. Use some or all of the following subjects to explain your answer to the question:

YOUR FAVORITES - What do like most? What's your favorite color? Food? Movie? Book?

YOUR INTERESTS - What are your hobbies? Why do you find them interesting? What would you like to learn more about? Why? What sport do you like to play? Watch?

YOUR SELF-TALK - What do you think about? Are you optimistic or pessimistic? Do you feel that you control your mind or does your mind control you?

YOUR HUMAN NEEDS - Are your needs being satisfied in your life right now? Who is helping to satisfy your human needs and how are they doing this? Who is hurting your satisfaction of the different human needs and how are they doing this?

YOUR VALUES - What is important to you? What are you against? How will your beliefs affect the direction you go in life? Give examples of how your values influence your decisions.

YOUR EMOTIONS - What emotions can you express openly? Which ones do you hide and why? How are you feeling about yourself and your life right now?

YOUR FRUSTRATIONS - What are you sick and tired of? How would you change things if you could?

YOUR FEARS - What are you afraid of at this moment in your life? Who are you afraid of? What are you afraid to do? What are you afraid is going to happen?

YOUR MANIPULATIONS - Do you ever act like someone other than your true self? When do you do this and why? Do you ever try to control the way somebody thinks or acts? Who? Why do you manipulate people and situations? What are you after?

YOUR HEALTH - How do you look after yourself? Where do you fail in regards to taking care of your body?

YOUR DECISIONS - Do you have any decisions that need to be made that will affect your future? What are your choices and what do you plan on doing?

YOUR GOALS - What are your goals for the next couple of years? What do you want your life to look like ten years from today? What distracts you from reaching your goals? What motivates you to keep going?

YOUR RELATIONSHIPS - Are you surrounded by people who love and support you? Who are they and why are they special to you?

YOUR FUTURE - What kind of impact do you want to make in this world? What influence do you believe you can have on others in your lifetime through your career choice or by just being you?

Some of these will take paragraphs to answer and some will take just lines. All of your responses need to be honest if you want this exercise to be of any value to you. Ponder, dwell, contemplate, and make your answer to "Who am I?" be a true reflection of the real you. This is something you just might reread a time or two in the next few years and maybe someday give to your own teenager and say, "Here. This was me when I was your age."

smile inside

Celebration Day

Participants will celebrate their social connections and achievements.

materials *Certificates of Appreciation* (p. 151) or personal achievement awards for each participant, journals, pens

1. Celebrate the completion of the course with a ceremony, meal, party, or all three.

2. Distribute *Certificates of Appreciation* to all participants for their *Make a Change Challenge* (p. 150) projects if completed, or distribute unique awards that celebrate every individual.

3. Conduct the second session of *Who Will Be...?* (p. 157), *Circle of Silence* (p. 158), *Psychiatrist* (p. 159), *Symbolic Gifts* (p. 160), or the group's favorite games if desired.

4. Reveal the answers to all the riddles from the Problem Solving and Decision Making module (p. 91) if you have not done so already.

5. Allow some free time so the participants have a chance to sign each other's journals.

smile inside

Who Will Be...?

Participants will suggest potential career options or creative pursuits for their peers according to what they have learned throughout their time together. They will guess which suggestions match each person in the group and discuss how they feel about others' perceptions of them.

materials   a list of everyone's names for each participant, pens, prepared handouts for the second session only

1. Hand out a list of everyone's names to each participant. Ask the group to suggest potential career options or creative outlets for each person based on what they have learned about that person during their time together. Ask the group to think about how each individual could achieve their greatest potential in life.

2. Examine the results in between sessions and create a *Who Will Be...?* handout that includes the most common and/or most humorous responses from the group. The following is an example:

> ## Who Will Be...
>
> A medical specialist helping third-world children?
>
> The author of a best-selling mystery novel?
>
> A professional soccer player in Spain?
>
> A lawyer and motivational speaker?
>
> A famous artist with a gold medal in cycling?
>
> "Father of the Year" to thirteen children?
>
> A fashion designer out of Paris?
>
> An internationally known band director?
>
> A video game designer?
>
> The owner of a wildlife sanctuary?

3. At the beginning of the second session, pass out the prepared *Who Will Be...?* handouts. Have participants match the names of their peers with the proposed vocations.

4. Share the answers on the prepared list and discuss the results of the activity with the participants.

5. Ask the group:

   - How many of you got all of the answers correct? How many missed only a few?
   - How do you feel about the way some of your peers perceived you?
   - Who thinks those plans are definitely in your future?

smile inside

Circle of Silence

Participants will maintain positive eye contact with each other. They will reflect on their experiences through discussion.

1. Split the participants into two even groups.

2. Have group one form a circle with their backs facing the center.

3. Have group two form a circle around group one facing the center, so each individual is face to face with another individual.

4. Ask each participant to look directly into the eyes of the person in front of him or her.

5. Tell them to maintain positive, sincere eye contact with the person across from them for as long as possible. This means no squinting, funny faces or intimidating staring.

6. After thirty to sixty seconds, tell the group in the outer circle to move clockwise so everyone has a new partner.

7. Once everyone has returned to their starting position, allow time for reflection. Ask the group:

   - How did this activity make you feel?
   - Would anyone like to share your experience?
   - How different was your experience with each person?
   - How did you manage to keep your focus?
   - Did anyone have a difficult time with this activity?
   - What were you thinking?
   - Did you only pay attention to the physical or did you see past that?
   - Have you ever looked into someone's eyes for that long? When and why?
   - What do you believe were the benefits of doing this activity?

smile inside

Psychiatrist

Participants will be tested on their knowledge of their peers.

> This game is best played after a group spends a lot of time together. It tests the group members on how well they got to know each other on a personal level. It also brings a lot of laughter so it's an ideal culminating activity.

1. Have the group sit in a circle. Nominate one or two psychiatrists—preferably outgoing people who will ask lots of creative questions and not abandon the task due to frustration. The psychiatrists will need to discover the secrets of the game.

2. Ask the psychiatrists to leave the room, then explain the secrets of the game to the remaining participants, who will act as the patients:

   - The psychiatrists will ask you, the patients, questions. Everyone must answer all questions as if you were the person to your left, but do not count the psychiatrists as part of the circle.
   - Anyone who knows that someone's answer is incorrect must say, "psychiatrist!" The game works best when the person on the left waits to see if anyone else in the group calls out "psychiatrist!" first.)
   - When someone says, "psychiatrist!" everyone must stand and find a new seat which alters your "personalities."
   - If you are asked your name, you must respond, "I'm Patient" so you don't give away the secret.

3. Bring the psychiatrists back into the room, invite them to sit in the circle, and give them their task:

   You are in charge of a therapy session. Ask the patients questions to discover their problems. Make eye contact before you address each patient. Your goal is to figure out three things:

   - What's going on with all the patients? (They're answering as if they were the people to their left.)
   - Why do the patients say, "psychiatrist!"? (An answer is incorrect.)
   - Why do the patients switch seats? (To change the people they are answering for in order to confuse the psychiatrists.)

4. Suggest questions for the psychiatrists to ask, such as:

   - What did you eat for lunch today?
   - Why are you wearing (a ring, a necklace, etc.)?
   - What sport do you like to play?
   - How many siblings do you have?

5. Allow the game to continue until the psychiatrists figure out what's going on. If they have difficulty, give them hints:

   - Why are the patients answering the questions the way they are?
   - How are they formulating their answers?
   - All the patients have the same "problem."
   - Ask everyone the same question.

smile inside

Symbolic Gifts

Participants will share what gift they would give to each
person in the group if there were no limitations.

1. Create a comfortable circle conducive to sharing.

2. Focusing on one individual at a time, allow every person or just a few share what they would give to that person if there were no limitations and why.

3. Let the process continue around the circle, keeping a consistent time limit for each person.

4. Encourage participants to be positive during this activity. Let them know that humor is acceptable, but the goal is to help everyone feel valued and uplifted.

smile inside

smile inside

20000211R00097

Made in the USA
Charleston, SC
22 June 2013